HOW TO FEEL

ANCIENT WISDOM FOR MODERN READERS

■ ■ ■ ■

For a full list of titles in the series, go to https://press.princeton.edu/series/ancient-wisdom-for-modern-readers.

How to Feel: An Ancient Guide to Minding Our Emotions by The Buddha

How to Be Caring: An Ancient Guide to a Compassionate Life by Shantideva

How to Cope: An Ancient Guide to Enduring Hardship by Boethius

How to Make a Home: An Ancient Guide to Style and Comfort by Vitruvius and Guests

How to Have Willpower: An Ancient Guide to Not Giving In by Plutarch and Prudentius

How to Talk about Love: An Ancient Guide for Modern Lovers by Plato

How to Eat: An Ancient Guide for Healthy Living by a Buffet of Ancient Authors

How to Lose Yourself: An Ancient Guide to Letting Go by the Buddha and His Followers

How to Be Queer: An Ancient Guide to Sexuality by Sappho, Plato, and Other Lovers

How to Get Over a Breakup: An Ancient Guide to Moving On by Ovid

How to Make Money: An Ancient Guide to Wealth Management by Pliny & Co.

HOW TO FEEL

■ ■ ■ ■ ■

An Ancient Guide to Minding Our Emotions

The Buddha

Selected, translated, and introduced by Maria Heim

PRINCETON UNIVERSITY PRESS
PRINCETON AND OXFORD

Published by Princeton University Press
41 William Street, Princeton, New Jersey 08540
99 Banbury Road, Oxford OX2 6JX

press.princeton.edu

GPSR Authorized Representative: Easy Access System Europe - Mustamäe tee 50, 10621 Tallinn, Estonia, gpsr.requests@easproject.com

ISBN 978-0-691-26739-5
ISBN (e-book) 978-0-691-26740-1

Library of Congress Control Number 2025936321

British Library Cataloging-in-Publication Data is available

Editorial: Rob Tempio and Chloe Coy
Production Editorial: Jill Harris
Text / Jacket Design: Heather Hansen
Production: Erin Suydam
Publicity: William Pagdatoon and Charlotte Coyne

Jacket image: Indian Museum Sculpture - Consolation of Ananda at Gijjhakuta, Jamalgarhi.

This book has been composed in Stempel Garamond and Adobe Text Pro with Futura Std

Printed in the United States of America

1 3 5 7 9 10 8 6 4 2

MIX
Paper | Supporting responsible forestry
FSC® C008955
FSC www.fsc.org

For Charlie

CONTENTS

PREFACE

Now, *it is for one who feels* that I proclaim:
This is suffering, the origin of suffering, its ceasing, and the path leading to its fading away.

—*AṄGUTTARA NIKĀYA* 1.176

Two and a half millennia ago, a teacher in north India known to his followers as the Buddha, the "Awakened One," addressed his teachings to people who feel—that is, to everyone. As beings who feel, we are vulnerable: we experience acute and chronic pain, both physical and mental. We are subject to addiction, anxiety, and depression.

We long for stability in a world of change. We hope that our loved ones will not be taken from us in death, accident, or circumstance, and yet, eventually, they are. We watch our own bodies and minds deteriorate and, ultimately, we face our own deaths.

To be sure, we also have pleasant and happy experiences, and we relish them. Yet even the highest transports of sensory pleasure prove impossible to secure permanently. They don't last, and even if they did, we would crave novelty and become restless and bored with them. Moreover, pleasures are sources and causes of suffering—honey on a razor's blade—as we often get attached to them and do stupid and immoral things to acquire them. They can distract us from what is truly important.

This condition of vulnerability to pain and suffering and to the pain of not being able to secure lasting happiness, came to be identified by the Buddha as *dukkha*, a term we can translate as "suffering" or "stress." The Buddha's simple, but also deep and existential, diagnosis of this vulnerability—"this is suffering"—became the cornerstone of his doctrine, the First Noble Truth in what he called the Four Noble Truths.

If the Buddha's teachings had ended there, things would be bleak. But the teachings get increasingly optimistic after this. The Second Noble Truth names the "origin" of suffering, namely, that it comes from craving. We suffer because we get caught up in our desires and in recurrent cycles of gratification and loss. To spot the cause of a condition is to begin to see how it can end. In fact, one can be rid of craving and so no longer controlled by it. This is the Third Noble Truth, that suffering can cease. The name for this ceasing is *nirvana*, the end of all suffering and the end of all toxic and negative emotions.

Finally, the prescription, the Fourth Noble Truth, is the way leading to the fading away of suffering. The Noble Eightfold Path is that way, and it includes eight mutually reinforcing practices of wisdom, conduct, and meditation that bring about freedom from suffering, that is, the achievement of nirvana. These are: right view, right intention, right speech, right action, right livelihood, right effort, right mindfulness, and right concentration.

These four truths are the Buddha's doctrine in a nutshell. And they are centered on what it is to feel.

INTRODUCTION

The teachings gathered here are addressed to real human beings—us—who feel, and who, when we stop and closely watch our feelings, find that they drive much of what we do. The selections of Buddhist teachings from the Pali Canon translated in this book offer both a deep exploration of human psychology and a meditation manual. They center on a category of human experience best translated as "feelings." This category includes the hedonic tones of experience—pleasant, painful, or neutral—as well as other phenomena that have such tones, including those that speakers of contemporary English would call "emotions." This book is a guide to noticing how one feels in order to change it fundamentally.

An Exploration of Human Psychology

Buddhist thinkers engaged in some of the deepest and most systematic practices of introspection available in the historical record. Ancient thinkers did not analyze or categorize their experience in the same way that moderns do. Wise people in different times have examined their experience closely and developed ways of describing it that differ from contemporary psychological categories and models. The Buddha and his followers developed a rich vocabulary to analyze experience, along with certain therapeutic programs to change it. While their analyses can be understood by modern people through translation and study and can intersect with certain scientific understandings being developed today, they are resistant to being entirely assimilated into modern categories. This is a good thing, and here's why.

Neuroscientists are increasingly showing that English categories like "emotions" used in contemporary psychology labs are not "natural kinds," that is, phenomena that are given to us by nature and that exist independently of our perception of them. Rather, emotions are socially constructed categories, fashioned by the complex interplay of brain, body, experience, culture, and language. Once we learn such categories in childhood, they are reinforced by neural pathways that make it seem as though they are simply givens of our human endowment.[1] But in fact emotions differ significantly across cultures and languages. Linguists also doubt that English ways of describing experience carve nature at the joints.[2] That Buddhist thinkers looked very closely into experience and came up with quite different ways of analyzing and classifying it can trouble modern English and modern psychology's supposed universalism. They can also give us alternatives that help us get out of the conceptual cages delimited by modern English and the psychological paradigms based on it.

In Buddhist texts, feeling (*vedanā*) refers to what we feel, undergo, experience, and recognize as having a valence or affective tone. It thus can mean simply "valence," the pleasant, painful, and neutral tones we can detect in all experiences. But it can also refer to certain phenomena—thoughts, aptitudes, faculties—that have these valences, and in this sense, it overlaps to some degree with the category of emotion. We will see in the pages ahead various ways that feelings were noticed and categorized.

The noticing is important: feelings are noticed by those feeling them—"I am feeling a pleasurable feeling" or "I am feeling a painful feeling."[3] There are a lot of sensations that we experience that we are not aware of, or at least we are not aware of until we attend to them. A stressful day may include tension in the neck even if one does not notice it. I have sensations of the bottom of my feet pressing against my shoes, but unless I notice them as such, they do not become "feelings." But when one feels these sensations *and* is aware that one is feeling them, one can be said to have these feelings.

As a category of instances that we, at least in part, construct by identifying them, "feelings" are not single phenomenon with a distinctive biological signature or fingerprint or essence. The pain of burning one's tongue on the too-hot morning coffee and the anguish of losing a good friend are both "painful feelings," but they are quite different experiences with no single essence. The pain feels different in each. Nevertheless, Buddhist thinkers found it helpful to note and categorize positive, negative, and neutral valences because it aided their goal of ridding us of the suffering and pain in human life. When one attends to the valences of experience, one can learn to manage and alleviate them.

A Meditation Manual

As much as the teachings translated here provide the modern world with a fresh psychological and philosophical analysis of experience, the texts were first and foremost practical and therapeutic in nature. Buddhist therapies of experience entail learning to attend to what is present, that is, to practice meta-awareness or "mindfulness" in becoming curious about, and aware of, the nature and contents of one's awareness. Meta-awareness is a crucial first step in addressing the suffering Buddhism aims to eradicate. When feelings as feelings are carefully tracked, they can be managed directly, chiefly by paying attention to what causes them and where they, in turn, lead. If we discover that certain states consistently bring us pain, we can work to replace them with others. Because of this, many of the passages in this book involve meditation techniques that slow one down enough to watch, moment-by-moment, what arises in the field of experience, what caused it, and what it, in turn, generates.

The word "watch" (*anupassati*) means, literally, *watching-while-following*: one witnesses and registers what happens as it happens and directly contemplates it. A central meditation practice alluded to in our selections (and often used in modern mindfulness practices) is the four "applications of mindfulness"—watching the body in the body, feeling in feelings, mind in mind, and phenomena in phenomena. That is, instead of just experiencing life with and through body, feeling, mind, and other phenomena, one turns them into the *objects* of one's attention.

In the first application, one slows down and observes bodily states like the breath and the body's postures and positions. One troubled with lust or vanity may go further to notice disgusting things about the body and its parts, or dwell on its inevitable decay and eventual death. These techniques can lead to disenchantment with the desires related to our bodies.

Moving on from the body, the "applications of mindfulness" practice turns to watching "feeling in feelings," using many of the practices we will see in the pages that follow. One observes how feelings come and go, much like winds passing through the sky, or travelers lodging at a guest house. By watching feelings and emotions come and go, we see their insubstantial nature and can stop giving them more power over us than they need to have. Watching them can free us from painful experiences by helping us see the causes, conditions, and contingency of feelings and how we might disengage from them.

The practice is then applied to "watching mind in mind." One directs one's attention to what is present in one's awareness as a whole, noting in particular how desire, hatred, and delusion are present, how they operate, and how they constrict and distract us. Onc also attends to what becomes possible when one disengages from these toxic experiences. Finally, the last application of mindfulness is the contemplation of "phenomena in phenomena." This practice deploys technical vocabulary that Buddhists developed to notice some of the most fine-grained bits of experience, such as the workings of sense desires, restlessness, regret, doubt, and lethargy that can hinder one's progress in meditation by clouding or agitating the mind.

Collectively these applications of mindfulness are said to be the path "for purifying beings, for overcoming grief and lamentation, for the subsiding of pain and distress, for finding the way, and for realizing nirvana."[4] They purify humans of toxic and painful experiences. This idea proclaims the Buddha's optimism that one can reach a way of being—nirvana—that is free of all suffering, desire, hatred, and delusion. As we will see in the selections gathered here on feelings, the techniques developed to eradicate suffering lead to increasingly sublime modes of happiness that transcend craving and sensory pleasure altogether and culminate in serenity and balance.

Paradoxes of Pleasure and Pain

One feature of the progression from suffering to nirvana is that one comes to see that even pleasant feeling (*sukha*) can be a kind of pain (*dukkha*). This idea has already been suggested in the First Noble Truth, that even the pleasurable and happy moments we are able to snatch in life are ephemeral and subject to loss. When our first son graduated from high school, we celebrated and I felt happy; but the happiness had a slight tinge of loss and sadness as I was simultaneously aware of his transition from boyhood into adulthood, his impending departure for college, and the unremitting passing of time. In this specific sense, even highly pleasant moments are tinged with *dukkha*, suffering, pain, and stress.

At the same time, the subsiding of all *dukkha* is also said to be a kind of sublime pleasure, happiness, or bliss. There is a paradox here, one that is articulated in the Buddhist sources themselves. Consider this passage spoken by two monks (both called by their honorifics "Venerables"):

> On one occasion the Venerable Sariputta was staying at Squirrel Park in the Bamboo Grove. There he addressed the monks: "Pleasure, friends, is this nirvana, pleasure, friends, is this nirvana!"
>
> When this was uttered, Venerable Udayi asked Sariputta: "But Sariputta, what

> pleasure could there be when nothing is felt here?"
>
> "Just this, friend, is the pleasure here, here where nothing is felt."[5]

This sublime paradox depends in part on the multivocality of the original language of the early discourses, Pali. The term in question, *sukha* (in some ways the opposite of *dukkha*), means pleasure or pleasant feeling. But it can also mean ease, happiness, and bliss. Nirvana, often referred to as "awakening" or "enlightenment," is characterized as the subsiding of the pushes and pulls endlessly jerking us around as we seek to gratify our desires and dodge what is disagreeable, the very subsiding of which is a supreme kind of pleasure or bliss.

The translator might thus be tempted to toggle back and forth in translating *sukha*, rendering it as "pleasure" when it refers to the pleasant sensory feelings one is aiming to eradicate, and switching to "happiness" or "bliss" when it refers to the state of being beyond sensory feeling altogether. This would be an appropriate translational choice, and one I am tempted to make. But to do so hides the playful and paradoxical quality that is evident in the original teachings. The passages themselves let these paradoxes stand: the highest pleasure is a state beyond pain and pleasure.

And perhaps there really is no paradox here. After all, the highest spiritual goal is not to become an automaton who feels nothing. Rather, it is to step out of the cycle of gratification and loss—what modern scientists call the systems of "reward-based learning" or "operant conditioning," that are based on positive and negative reinforcement and drive so much of what we do. What remains are the sublime happinesses evoked in the Buddhist texts translated in this book.

More about the Buddha

"The Buddha" is a title or achievement claimed by a teacher who lived sometime between the 6th and the 4th centuries BCE (firm dates are hard to come by in ancient Indian history). His name was Siddhartha Gautama as it is known in Sanskrit, or Siddhattha Gotama in the Pali language used in this book. While scholars believe he was an historical person who founded a religious order of celibate monks (here, I am using "monks" to refer to both male and female monastics), we know little of his life independently of the texts themselves and the legends that grew up around them.

According to those legends, Siddhattha was born a prince and was expected to become a great emperor. But as a young man he came to be acutely aware of the suffering of illness, aging, and death, and of the deeper psychological patterns perpetuating suffering in human life. This led him to renounce the world and join other yogis, ascetics, and monastics who sought the solution to life's pain and confusion in the quiet austerity of the forests, unencumbered by the distractions of household life. After years of training under various gurus and engaging in sometimes quite extreme experiments with bodily mortification, Siddhattha struck out on his own, developing his own methods for observing experience until he achieved, over the course of one dramatic night under a magnificent *ficus* tree, a breakthrough—nirvana, the end of all suffering.

The insight he attained on the night of awakening is mentioned in a passage in our book as it bears on feeling. The Buddha claims that "with regard to things not heard before, vision arose, knowledge arose, understanding arose, wisdom arose, and clarity arose" with respect to how feeling works.

The Texts and the Translations

The texts translated here are selections from the Pali Canon. The Pali Canon was one of the earliest collections of Buddhist scriptures and the most complete corpus surviving in an Indian language. (Pali is an ancient Buddhist language related to Sanskrit). These scriptures are revered to this day by Theravada Buddhists. The Canon is considered to be the "words of the Buddha," although, like other thinkers of the time, the Buddha did not write down his teachings. The large body of material attributed to him was said to be transmitted through mnemonic techniques by his disciples and their followers for centuries before it was written down.

The centerpiece of this book is a chapter from *Connected Discourses* (*Saṃyutta Nikāya*), one of the main collections in the Canon. Chapter Two, "Teachings on Feelings" (*Vedanāsaṃyutta*), brings together under the theme of feelings (*vedanā*) passages scattered elsewhere in the Canon. These passages convey the Buddha's sermons and his dialogues with disciples and rival ascetics.

The purpose of *Connected Discourses* is to gather passages found across the many volumes of the Buddha's teachings into thematic chapters, aiming for thoroughness rather than conciseness. Because it is a collection of passages, the chapter has a lot of repetition. I have preserved some of the repetition in the translation, since the passages' repetitive qualities are part of the meditation practices they enact (though I omit most of the verbatim repetitions). Repeated refrains invite readers to slow down and watch, moment-by-moment, their own experience, attending to and noting each phenomenon, pattern, and nuance as they occur. The reader will return, time and again, to the three kinds of feelings, pleasant, painful, and neutral (literally, "neither pleasant nor painful"), a cadence that serves as a kind of steady and melodic baseline throughout the piece. Passages go from there to develop attention to further dimensions and possibilities in the field of experience.

"Teachings on Feelings" is flanked by short selections from other canonical books that I could not resist including. We begin in Chapter One with a teaching that describes Siddhattha exploring his experience prior to his awakening when he was a "bodhisatta," (that is, a Buddha-in-training), on the way to his breakthrough but not quite there yet. In "Two Kinds of Thoughts," we encounter him classifying his experiences in two categories, based on what they bring about. Simply by watching his thoughts and seeing where they would go, Siddhattha realized a key insight, namely that the mind "comes to be inclined towards whatever it frequently ponders and thinks about." Our minds are created by what we allow them to dwell on. And we have tremendous agency and choice about this—we can choose what to dwell on and what to let go, guarding our minds against harmful thoughts and feelings and inviting them into more positive states.

The short passage translated in Chapter Three, "Four Immeasurables," explores some of the highly positive states in which one can dwell when one relinquishes the harmful thoughts and feelings associated with anger, hate, envy, cruelty, and apathy. The text celebrates the spaciousness and freedom of four immeasurable "sublime attitudes" that become possible when one lets go of toxic emotions toward others that, left to themselves, constrict and distort one's experience. These are varieties of love and peace—namely, lovingkindness, compassion, sympathetic joy, and equanimity—that emerge when we direct our attention to others without the barriers of negative emotions. They are "immeasurables" in that one can always develop them further.

The final excerpt in Chapter Four, which I call "An Upward Spiral," is one of the most sublime psychological teachings in the Pali Canon. Many of the practices we are studying in this book involve removing harmful states. Often this is enough—the sheer absence of greed, hatred, delusion, ill will, sensual desire, cruelty, and so on, frees us of their agitations, distortions, and constraints and makes way for love, calmness, clarity, and freedom to emerge in their place. This final chapter outlines a natural progression from removing harmful actions and thoughts to the supreme happiness and freedom that Buddhism holds out as possible for human beings.

To orient beginning students of Buddhism and ease their way into these teachings, I offer brief explanatory remarks before each passage or pair of passages. There are also technical terms that can be found in the Glossary with a full explanation.

HOW TO FEEL

TWO KINDS OF THOUGHTS

Our first selection shows methods that the Buddha, even before he became the Buddha, developed to watch the patterns of his experience. Here he watches his thoughts, turning them into objects of scrutiny and then dividing them into two piles, based on his direct empirical experience of whether and how they lead to harm.

This mindfulness practice of noticing and observing what occurs can help one relate to one's experiences differently by becoming disenchanted with harmful experiences and casually observant of, but not overly stimulated by, beneficial ones.

Most of us have addictions—to obvious substances like tobacco, drugs, alcohol, and food, as well as to our phones, to our compulsive habits of mind, and even to ourselves.[1] *Our brains are formed by reward-based learning, where we fall into habits based on positive and negative reinforcement. When we step back from these and observe their reinforcing cycles of craving and gratification, we can grow disenchanted. Neuroscientists and psychiatrists have begun to show that certain mindfulness practices based on the Pali Canon are remarkably effective in treating addiction because they address these reward-based systems by careful and curious attention to how they feel.*[2]

I invite the reader to notice the structure of this passage, wherein thoughts have their opposites. Thoughts of sensual desire, ill will, and cruelty can be replaced by, respectively, "letting things go" (disengaging from or renouncing sense desires), "lack of ill will" (which can include kindness but also experiences simply lacking anger and malice), and "noncruelty" (thoughts free of any desire to harm oneself or others). Pervading one's experience and habits with kinder and gentler thoughts crowds out their opposites and reshapes one's inclinations. The brain has its ruts and habits. But it is also plastic, and we can gradually restructure its neural pathways.

A final insight of the passage is that for all their beneficial qualities, even thoughts lacking sensual desire, ill will, and cruelty can themselves become overstimulating when we ruminate on them. We can perseverate, addicted to our own thoughts and prone to whiling away time in daydreaming. Better to simply note their coming and going, permitting oneself to become calm, composed, and open, rather than getting drawn into them.

Dvedhāvitakkasuttaṃ
(Majjhima Nikāya i. 114–118)

Evaṃ me sutaṃ—ekaṃ samayaṃ bhagavā sāvatthiyaṃ viharati jetavane anāthapiṇḍikassa ārāme. Tatra kho bhagavā bhikkhū āmantesi—bhikkhavoti. Bhadante ti te bhikkhū bhagavato paccassosuṃ. Bhagavā etadavoca—

Pubbeva me, bhikkhave, sambodhā anabhisambuddhassa bodhisattasseva sato etadahosi—yaṃnūnāhaṃ dvidhā katvā dvidhā katvā vitakke vihareyyanti. So kho ahaṃ, bhikkhave, yo cāyaṃ kāmavitakko yo ca byāpādavitakko yo ca vihiṃsāvitakko—imaṃ ekaṃ bhāgamakāsiṃ; yo cāyaṃ nekkhammavitakko yo ca abyāpādavitakko yo ca avihiṃsāvitakko—imaṃ dutiyaṃ bhāgamakāsiṃ.

Thus have I heard. At one time the Buddha was staying at Jeta's Grove in Savatthi in Anathapindika's Park. There the Buddha addressed the monks: "Monks!"

"Yes, sir," the monks replied to the Buddha.

The Buddha said this: "Previously, monks, as an unenlightened bodhisatta prior to my awakening, I thought: *What if I were to spend time dividing my thoughts into two categories?* And so, monks, I placed on one side any thought of sensual desire, any thought of ill will, and any thought of cruelty. And I placed on a second side any thought of letting things go, any thought lacking ill will, and any thought lacking cruelty.

Tassa mayhaṃ, bhikkhave, evaṃ appamattassa ātāpino pahitattassa viharato uppajjati kāmavitakko. So evaṃ pajānāmi—uppanno kho me ayaṃ kāmavitakko. So ca kho attabyābādhāyapi saṃvattati, parabyābādhāyapi saṃvattati, ubhayabyābādhāyapi saṃvattati, paññānirodhiko vighātapakkhiko anibbānasaṃvattaniko. Attabyābādhāya saṃvattatītipi me, bhikkhave, paṭisañcikkhato abbhatthaṃ gacchati; parabyābādhāya saṃvattatītipi me, bhikkhave, paṭisañcikkhato abbhatthaṃ gacchati; ubhayabyābādhāya saṃvattatītipi me, bhikkhave, paṭisañcikkhato abbhatthaṃ gacchati; paññānirodhiko vighātapakkhiko anibbānasaṃvattanikotipi me, bhikkhave, paṭisañcikkhato abbhatthaṃ gacchati. So kho ahaṃ, bhikkhave, uppannuppannaṃ kāmavitakkaṃ pajahameva byantameva naṃ akāsiṃ.

"While I was spending my time with care, effort, and determination, a thought of sensual desire occurred in me. I understood it in this way: *This thought of sensual desire has occurred in me. It surely leads to my own harm, leads to another's harm, or leads to harm for both of us; it obstructs wisdom, causes trouble, and leads away from nirvana.* Monks, for one reflecting, *This leads to my own harm*, it comes to an end. Monks, for one reflecting, *This leads to another's harm*, it comes to an end. Monks, for one reflecting, *This leads to harm for both of us*, it comes to an end. Monks, for one reflecting, *This obstructs wisdom, causes trouble, and leads away from nirvana*, it comes to an end. And in fact, monks, whenever a thought of sensual desire occurred, I just let it go, abandoned it, and brought it to an end.

Tassa mayhaṃ, bhikkhave, evaṃ appamattassa ātāpino pahitattassa viharato uppajjati byāpādavitakko . . . pe . . . uppajjati vihiṃsāvitakko. So evaṃ pajānāmi—uppanno kho me ayaṃ vihiṃsāvitakko. So ca kho attabyābādhāyapi saṃvattati, parabyābādhāyapi saṃvattati, ubhayabyābādhāyapi saṃvattati, paññānirodhiko vighātapakkhiko anibbānasaṃvattaniko. Attabyābādhāya saṃvattatītipi me, bhikkhave, paṭisañcikkhato abbhatthaṃ gacchati; parabyābādhāya saṃvattatītipi me, bhikkhave, paṭisañcikkhato abbhatthaṃ gacchati; ubhayabyābādhāya saṃvattatītipi me, bhikkhave, paṭisañcikkhato abbhatthaṃ gacchati; paññānirodhiko vighātapakkhiko anibbānasaṃvattaniko tipi me, bhikkhave, paṭisañcikkhato abbhatthaṃ gacchati. So kho ahaṃ, bhikkhave, uppannuppannaṃ vihiṃsāvitakkaṃ pajahameva vinodameva byantameva naṃ akāsiṃ.

"While I was spending my time with care, effort, and determination, a thought of ill will occurred in me, and then a cruel thought occurred. In each case, I understood it in this way: *This cruel thought has occurred in me. It surely leads to my own harm, leads to another's harm, or leads to harm for both of us; it obstructs wisdom, causes trouble, and leads away from nirvana.* Monks, for one reflecting, *This leads to my own harm*, it comes to an end. Monks, for one reflecting, *This leads to another's harm*, it comes to an end. Monks, for one reflecting, *This leads to harm for both of us*, it comes to an end. Monks, for one reflecting, *This obstructs wisdom, causes trouble, and leads away from nirvana*, it comes to an end. And in fact, monks, whenever a cruel thought occurred, I just let it go, abandoned it, and brought it to an end.

Yaññadeva, bhikkhave, bhikkhu bahulamanuvitakketi anuvicāreti, tathā tathā nati hoti cetaso. Kāmavitakkaṃ ce, bhikkhave, bhikkhu bahulamanuvitakketi anuvicāreti, pahāsi nekkhammavitakkaṃ, kāmavitakkaṃ bahulamakāsi, tassa taṃ kāmavitakkāya cittaṃ namati. Byāpādavitakkaṃ ce, bhikkhave . . . pe . . . vihiṃsāvitakkaṃ ce, bhikkhave, bhikkhu bahulamanuvitakketi anuvicāreti, pahāsi avihiṃsāvitakkaṃ, vihiṃsāvitakkaṃ bahulamakāsi, tassa taṃ vihiṃsāvitakkāya cittaṃ namati.

Seyyathāpi, bhikkhave, vassānaṃ pacchime māse saradasamaye kiṭṭhasambādhe gopālako gāvo rakkheyya. So tā gāvo tato tato daṇḍena ākoṭeyya paṭikoṭeyya sannirundheyya sannivāreyya. Taṃ kissa hetu? Passati hi so, bhikkhave, gopālako tatonidānaṃ vadhaṃ vā bandhanaṃ vā jāniṃ vā garahaṃ vā. Evameva

"Monks, a monk's mind comes to be inclined towards whatever it frequently ponders and thinks about. A monk who frequently ponders and thinks thoughts of sensual desire has abandoned thoughts of letting things go and developed thoughts of sensual desire, and so inclines the mind to thoughts of sensual desire. So too with thoughts of ill will and cruel thoughts. A monk who frequently ponders and thinks cruel thoughts has abandoned kind thoughts and developed cruel thoughts, and so inclines the mind to cruel thoughts.

"Consider, monks, a cowherd guarding cattle in the last month of the rainy season, the autumn harvest time when the crops are full. From all sides, he would strike, beat back, block, and keep the cows away with a stick. For what reason? The cowherd sees, monks, the punishment, imprisonment,

kho ahaṃ, bhikkhave, addasaṃ akusalānaṃ dhammānaṃ ādīnavaṃ okāraṃ saṃkilesaṃ, kusalānaṃ dhammānaṃ nekkhamme ānisaṃsaṃ vodānapakkhaṃ.

Tassa mayhaṃ, bhikkhave, evaṃ appamattassa ātāpino pahitattassa viharato uppajjati nekkhammavitakko. So evaṃ pajānāmi—uppanno kho me ayaṃ nekkhammavitakko. So ca kho nevattabyābādhāya saṃvattati, na parabyābādhāya saṃvattati, na ubhayabyābādhāya saṃvattati, paññāvuddhiko avighātapakkhiko nibbānasaṃvattaniko'. Rattiṃ cepi naṃ, bhikkhave, anuvitakkeyyaṃ anuvicāreyyaṃ, neva tatonidānaṃ bhayaṃ samanupassāmi. Divasaṃ cepi naṃ, bhikkhave, anuvitakkeyyaṃ anuvicāreyyaṃ, neva tatonidānaṃ bhayaṃ samanupassāmi. Rattindivaṃ cepi naṃ, bhikkhave, anuvitakkeyyaṃ

loss, and scolding that would occur on their account. Similarly, monks, I saw the drawbacks, the inferiority, and problematic nature of bad states, and in letting them go, I saw the benefits and purifying power of good states.

"While I was spending my time with care, effort, and determination, a thought of letting things go occurred in me. I understood it in this way: *This thought of letting things go has occurred in me. It does not lead to my own harm, does not lead to another's harm, and does not lead to harm for both of us; it amplifies wisdom, does not cause trouble, and leads toward nirvana.* Monks, if I were to ponder and think about it at night, I see nothing to fear from it. If I were to ponder and think about it by day, I see nothing to fear from it. And even were I to ponder and think about it night and day, I see nothing

anuvicāreyyaṃ, neva tatonidānaṃ bhayaṃ samanupassāmi. Api ca kho me aticiraṃ anuvitakkayato anuvicārayato kāyo kilameyya. Kāye kilante cittaṃ ūhaññeyya. Ūhate citte ārā cittaṃ samādhimhāti. So kho ahaṃ, bhikkhave, ajjhattameva cittaṃ saṇṭhapemi sannisādemi ekodiṃ karomi samādahāmi. Taṃ kissa hetu? 'Mā me cittaṃ ūhaññīti.

Tassa mayhaṃ, bhikkhave, evaṃ appamattassa ātāpino pahitattassa viharato uppajjati abyāpādavitakko . . . pe . . . uppajjati avihiṃsāvitakko. So evaṃ pajānāmi—uppanno kho me ayaṃ avihiṃsāvitakko. So ca kho nevattabyābādhāya saṃvattati, na parabyābādhāya saṃvattati, na ubhayabyābādhāya saṃvattati, paññāvuddhiko avighātapakkhiko nibbānasaṃvattaniko. Rattiṃ cepi naṃ, bhikkhave, anuvitakkeyyaṃ anuvicāreyyaṃ, neva tatonidānaṃ bhayaṃ samanupassāmi. Divasaṃ

to fear from it. And yet, pondering and thinking about it too much would tire the body. And when the body is tired, the mind gets overstimulated. And when the mind is overstimulated, it is far from concentrated. And so, monks, I steadied my mind internally, calmed it down, unified, and composed it. For what reason? So that my mind was not overstimulated.

"While I was spending my time with care, effort, and determination, a thought lacking ill will occurred in me, and an uncruel thought occurred. In each case, I understood it in this way: *This kind thought has occurred in me. It does not lead to my own harm, does not lead to another's harm, and does not lead to harm for both of us; it amplifies wisdom, does not cause trouble, and leads toward nirvana.* Monks, were I to ponder and think about it at night, I see

cepi naṃ, bhikkhave, anuvitakkeyyaṃ anuvicāreyyaṃ, neva tatonidānaṃ bhayaṃ samanupassāmi. Rattindivaṃ cepi naṃ, bhikkhave, anuvitakkeyyaṃ anuvicāreyyaṃ, neva tatonidānaṃ bhayaṃ samanupassāmi. Api ca kho me aticiraṃ anuvitakkayato anuvicārayato kāyo kilameyya. Kāye kilante cittaṃ ūhaññeyya. Ūhate citte ārā cittaṃ samādhimhāti. So kho ahaṃ, bhikkhave, ajjhattameva cittaṃ saṇṭhapemi, sannisādemi, ekodiṃ karomi samādahāmi. Taṃ kissa hetu? Mā me cittaṃ ūhaññīti.

Yaññadeva, bhikkhave, bhikkhu bahulamanuvitakketi anuvicāreti, tathā tathā nati hoti cetaso. Nekkhammavitakkañce, bhikkhave, bhikkhu bahulamanuvitakketi anuvicāreti, pahāsi kāmavitakkaṃ, nekkhammavitakkaṃ bahulamakāsi, tassaṃ taṃ nekkhammavitakkāya cittaṃ namati. Abyāpādavitakkañce,

nothing to fear from it. If I were to ponder and think about it by day, I see nothing to fear from it. And even were I to ponder and think about it night and day, I see nothing to fear from it. And yet, pondering and thinking about it too much would tire the body. And when the body is tired, the mind gets overstimulated. And when the mind is overstimulated, it is far from concentrated. And so, monks, I steadied my mind internally, calmed it down, focused and composed it. For what reason? So that my mind was not overstimulated.

"Monks, a monk's mind comes to be inclined towards whatever it frequently ponders and thinks about. A monk who frequently ponders and thinks thoughts of letting things go has abandoned thoughts of sensual desire and developed thoughts of letting things go, and so inclines the

bhikkhave . . . pe . . . avihiṃsāvitakkañce, bhikkhave, bhikkhu bahulamanuvitakketi anuvicāreti, pahāsi vihiṃsāvitakkaṃ, avihiṃsāvitakkaṃ bahulamakāsi, tassa taṃ avihiṃsāvitakkāya cittaṃ namati.

Seyyathāpi, bhikkhave, gimhānaṃ pacchime māse sabbasassesu gāmantasambhatesu gopālako gāvo rakkheyya, tassa rukkhamūlagatassa vā abbhokāsagatassa vā satikaraṇīyameva hoti—etā gāvoti. Evamevaṃ kho, bhikkhave, satikaraṇīyameva ahosi—ete dhammāti.

Āraddhaṃ kho pana me, bhikkhave, vīriyaṃ ahosi asallīnaṃ, upaṭṭhitā sati asammuṭṭhā, passaddho kāyo asāraddho, samāhitaṃ cittaṃ ekaggaṃ . . . . .

mind to thoughts of letting things go. So too with thoughts lacking ill will and cruelty, monks. A monk who frequently ponders and thinks kind thoughts has abandoned cruel thoughts and developed kind thoughts, and so inclines the mind to kind thoughts.

"Consider, monks, a cowherd guarding cattle in the last month of the hot season when all the crops have been harvested in the village. Hanging out at the foot of a tree or in the open air, it is enough for him to just be mindful that the cows are there. Similarly, monks, it is enough to just be mindful that these phenomena are there.

"Then, monks, unshaken energy was aroused in me, unclouded mindfulness was present, my body was calm and unruffled, and my mind, centered and unified."[3]

TEACHINGS ON FEELINGS

Our main selection, "Teachings on Feelings" begins with attending to the three valences—pleasant, painful, and neutral—and we will see it return to this phrasing time and again. Being mindful of them turns them into objects about which we can become curious. The context here is concentration, learning to meditate and become composed, mindful, and clearly comprehending everything that occurs within one's field of experience.

The first passage in this section is an echo of the Four Noble Truths, except that instead of "suffering" (dukkha) as the First Noble Truth, we are urged to notice "feelings." But the pattern of noting what is present, identifying its origin, knowing how it stops, and knowing the path to stopping it, is the same. The word "dukkha" means both "suffering" in general and "painful feeling" in particular, in ways that challenge the translator at many junctures in this text. To translate it as "suffering" picks up its resonance with the Four Noble Truths; to translate it as "painful feeling" indicates that it belongs to the category of instances that have a painful valence or tone in contrast to those that have a pleasant valence.

In the second passage, we confront a similar conundrum in translating sukha, a term that can mean pleasant feeling, as it does here, as well as ease, happiness, or bliss. In this teaching we start to see that even pleasant feeling is suffering—or painful—insofar as it is ephemeral and we will lose it. When we peer into the Pali texts and see the multivocality at work in these terms, we begin to see the Buddha challenge even our basic ideas about what we are experiencing.

Vedanāsaṃyuttaṃ
(selections from Saṃyutta Nikāya iv.204-237)

Samādhisuttaṃ

Tisso imā, bhikkhave, vedanā. Katamā tisso? Sukhā vedanā, dukkhā vedanā, adukkhamasukhā vedanā—imā kho, bhikkhave, tisso vedanāti.

Samāhito sampajāno, sato buddhassa
sāvako;
Vedanā ca pajānāti, vedanānañca
sambhavaṃ.

Yattha cetā nirujjhanti, maggañca
khayagāminaṃ;
Vedanānaṃ khayā bhikkhu, nicchāto
parinibbuto ti.

Concentration

"Monks, there are three kinds of feelings. What are the three? Pleasant feeling, painful feeling, and neutral feeling—these are the three kinds of feelings, monks.

A student of the Buddha, composed,
clearly comprehending, and mindful,
comes to know feelings, the origin of
feelings, where they cease, and the
path leading to their fading away.
With the fading away of feelings, a
monk is calmed and free of desire."

Sukhasuttaṃ

Tisso imā, bhikkhave, vedanā. Katamā tisso? Sukhā vedanā, dukkhā vedanā, adukkhamasukhā vedanā—imā kho, bhikkhave, tisso vedanāti.

Sukhaṃ vā yadi vā dukkhaṃ, adukkhama-
sukhaṃ saha;
Ajjhattañca bahiddhā ca, yaṃ kiñci atthi
veditaṃ.
Etaṃ dukkhanti ñatvāna, mosadhammaṃ
palokinaṃ;
Phussa phussa vayaṃ passaṃ, evaṃ tattha
virajjatīti.

Pleasure

"Monks, there are three kinds of feelings. What are the three? Pleasant feeling, painful feeling, and neutral feeling—these are the three kinds of feelings, monks.

> Recognizing that whatever is felt—
> whether pleasant, painful, neutral,
> one's own, or another's[1]—is suffering,
> deceptive, and perishable, one touches
> it again and again only to see it
> disintegrate.
> In this way, one loses interest in it."

▪▪▪

The next passage invites the reader to see that there are underlying tendencies at work in our feelings and that feelings are both generated by these tendencies and come to reinforce them. For example, we have latent proclivities that draw us toward pleasant things. And so, when we feel something pleasant, we generate desire for it; when we attain it, we are gratified, further reinforcing our tendencies for craving and desire. When we don't attain it, we are frustrated and often crave the object all the more or seek another form of gratification. When we feel pain, the object triggers the underlying tendency of aversion toward it as well as the tendency to crave a pleasurable distraction from it.

Even neutral feelings have an underlying tendency at work in them, which is ignorance, in that we don't usually attend to them and so are not fully aware of them. The feelings that are neither pleasant nor painful refer to much of our experience, that which simply presents as neutral or indeterminate. Brushing my teeth in the morning is neither pleasant nor painful; it just is, so I often do it rather mindlessly. The practices here would have us attend more closely to even these experiences.

But there is another referent to these neutral experiences: insofar as one achieves a state of not being caught up in the treadmill of reward-based pleasure and pain, one has a "peacefulness that is neither pleasant nor painful." This is the state of "equanimity," the mental balance and nonreactivity that allows for peace even in the face of pain. We find mention of this peacefulness in the passage below as a state that one may delight in (even while one should be cautioned that it is not to be mistaken for the highest release, which is nirvana).

Then, in "A Bottomless Abyss" we have a poignant illustration of pain and its depths that anyone in chronic or acute pain will readily recognize.

Pahānasuttaṃ

Tisso imā, bhikkhave, vedanā. Katamā tisso? Sukhā vedanā, dukkhā vedanā, adukkhamasukhā vedanā. Sukhāya, bhikkhave, vedanāya rāgānusayo pahātabbo, dukkhāya vedanāya paṭighānusayo pahātabbo, adukkhamasukhāya vedanāya avijjānusayo pahātabbo. Yato kho, bhikkhave, bhikkhuno sukhāya vedanāya rāgānusayo pahīno hoti, dukkhāya vedanāya paṭighānusayo pahīno hoti, adukkhamasukhāya vedanāya avijjānusayo pahīno hoti, ayaṃ vuccati, bhikkhave, bhikkhu niranusayo sammaddaso acchecchi taṇhaṃ, vivattayi saṃyojanaṃ, sammā mānābhisamayā antamakāsi dukkhassāti.

Giving Things Up

"Monks, there are three kinds of feelings. What are the three? Pleasant feeling, painful feeling, and neutral feeling. In relation to pleasant feeling, the underlying tendency of desire should be given up; in relation to painful feeling, the underlying tendency of aversion should be given up; and with respect to neutral feeling, the underlying tendency of ignorance should be given up. A monk who gives up the underlying tendency toward desire for pleasant feeling, who gives up the underlying tendency of aversion toward painful feeling, and who gives up the underlying tendency of ignorance toward neutral feeling, is said to be 'a monk free of underlying tendencies who sees rightly, cuts off craving, breaks the chains, completely cuts through conceit, and puts an end to suffering.'

Sukhaṃ vedayamānassa vedanaṃ
  appajānato;
So rāgānusayo hoti, anissaraṇadassino.
Dukkhaṃ vedayamānassa, vedanaṃ
  appajānato;
Paṭighānusayo hoti, anissaraṇadassino.
Adukkhamasukhaṃ santaṃ, bhūri-
  paññena desitaṃ;
Tañcāpi abhinandati, neva dukkhā
  pamuccati.
Yato ca bhikkhu ātāpī, sampajaññaṃ na
  riñcati;
Tato so vedanā sabbā, parijānāti paṇḍito.
So vedanā pariññāya, diṭṭhe dhamme
  anāsavo;
Kāyassa bhedā dhammaṭṭho, saṅkhyaṃ
  nopeti vedagū ti.

One feeling pleasure without fully
understanding feeling
has the underlying tendency of desire
and can see no escape.
One feeling pain without fully under-
standing feeling
has the underlying tendency of aversion
and can see no escape.
And one delighting even in the peaceful-
ness that is neither pleasant nor painful
taught by the one of great wisdom,
is still not released from suffering.
But a monk who is energetic, intelligent,
and clearly comprehending,
thoroughly understands all feelings.
One thoroughly understanding feelings
is free of destructive predispositions
in this life;
when the body gives way, one grounded
in truth possesses a knowledge that
cannot be calculated."

Pātālasuttaṃ

Assutavā, bhikkhave, puthujjano yaṃ vācaṃ bhāsati—atthi mahāsamudde pātālo ti. Taṃ kho panetaṃ, bhikkhave, assutavā puthujjano asantaṃ avijjamānaṃ evaṃ vācaṃ bhāsati—atthi mahāsamudde pātālo ti. Sārīrikānaṃ kho etaṃ, bhikkhave, dukkhānaṃ vedanānaṃ adhivacanaṃ yadidaṃ pātāloti. Assutavā, bhikkhave, puthujjano sārīrikāya dukkhāya vedanāya phuṭṭho samāno socati kilamati paridevati urattāḷiṃ kandati sammohaṃ āpajjati. Ayaṃ vuccati, bhikkhave, assutavā puthujjano pātāle na paccuṭṭhāsi, gādhañca nājjhagā. Sutavā ca kho, bhikkhave, ariyasāvako sārīrikāya dukkhāya vedanāya phuṭṭho samāno neva socati, na kilamati, na paridevati, na urattāḷiṃ kandati, na sammohaṃ āpajjati. Ayaṃ vuccati, bhikkhave, sutavā ariyasāvako pātāle paccuṭṭhāsi, gādhañca ajjhagā ti.

A Bottomless Abyss

"Monks, an uninformed ordinary person says such things as 'there is a bottomless abyss in the great ocean.' But the ordinary person who says this is saying something false and untrue. Rather, a 'bottomless abyss' is an expression for painful bodily feeling. An uninformed ordinary person who is being affected by a painful bodily feeling, grieves, gets exhausted, weeps, beats their breast, and becomes unhinged. This refers to the ordinary person who does not emerge from the bottomless abyss, and who does not gain a foothold. But the well-informed noble disciple who is affected by a painful bodily feeling does not grieve, get exhausted, weep, beat their breast, or become unhinged. This refers to the well-informed noble disciple who emerges from the bottomless abyss and gains a foothold.

Yo etā nādhivāseti, uppannā vedanā
dukhā;
Sārīrikā pāṇaharā, yāhi phuṭṭho
pavedhati.
Akkandati parodati, dubbalo
appathāmako;
Na so pātāle paccuṭṭhāsi, atho gādhampi
nājjhagā.
Yo cetā adhivāseti, uppannā vedanā
dukhā;
Sārīrikā pāṇaharā, yāhi phuṭṭho na
vedhati;
Sa ve pātāle paccuṭṭhāsi, atho gādhampi
ajjhagā ti.

Whoever cannot bear a painful, life-
 sapping bodily feeling as it arises,
trembles when touched, cries and
 laments,
and is weak and depleted of strength.
This one does not rise up out of the
 bottomless abyss
and does not even gain a foothold.
But whoever bears a painful, life-
 sapping bodily feeling as it arises,
does not tremble at the touch, and rises
 up out of the bottomless abyss
 to gain a foothold."

▪▪▪

The next two passages develop the metaphor of an arrow. The first passage states again that pleasant feelings should be seen as painful in the specific sense that they reinforce desire and craving, and are yet impermanent and so will inevitably frustrate those desires.

We are then introduced to the idea that painful feelings are like arrows. Some pain is inevitable in life. We are subject to physical harm and illness; we lose people we love; we will die. Such arrows or darts will strike us. But much of our pain is a second arrow that we shoot ourselves with by the way we respond to the first. We tend to take that initial pain personally. The mental pain, reactivity, and anguish we bring to our pain is the second arrow. There is a subtle psychological insight here: we can be attached to and invested in our pain in a way that amplifies it.

An example may help. Upon watching the final results of a consequential national election come in and finding that one's country has chosen a trajectory that one feels is dangerous for the nation and planet, one's heart may become gripped with shock, anger, and fear. There may be no easy way to avoid such feelings, at least at first, for those committed to and engaged in the world. But with training, the mind can learn to cease pointlessly ruminating on these emotions and torturing oneself with outrage and dread at 3:00 a.m. Coming to recognize that one is perversely attached to allowing one's sleep and peace of mind to yield to rage and anxiety can be the beginning of learning how to dissipate them. Learning to arrest a pattern of tormenting oneself with negative emotions can also clear the way for effective action when daylight dawns.

We are thus encouraged to see that we need not shoot the second arrow.

Daṭṭhabbasuttaṃ

Tisso imā, bhikkhave, vedanā. Katamā tisso? Sukhā vedanā, dukkhā vedanā, adukkhamasukhā vedanā. Sukhā, bhikkhave, vedanā dukkhato daṭṭhabbā, dukkhā vedanā sallato daṭṭhabbā, adukkhamasukhā vedanā aniccato daṭṭhabbā. Yato kho, bhikkhave, bhikkhuno sukhā vedanā dukkhato diṭṭhā hoti, dukkhā vedanā sallato diṭṭhā hoti, adukkhamasukhā vedanā aniccato diṭṭhā hoti—ayaṃ vuccati, bhikkhave, bhikkhu sammaddaso acchecchi taṇhaṃ, vivattayi saṃyojanaṃ, sammā mānābhisamayā antamakāsi dukkhassā ti.

Yo sukhaṃ dukkhato adda, dukkhamaddakkhi sallato;

What Should be Seen

"Monks, there are three kinds of feelings. What are the three? Pleasant feeling, painful feeling, and neutral feeling. Pleasant feeling should be seen as painful, painful feeling should be seen as an arrow, and neutral feeling should be seen as impermanent. When a monk sees a pleasant feeling as painful, a painful feeling as an arrow, and a neutral feeling as impermanent, this much can be said: 'Seeing correctly, the monk cuts off craving, breaks the chains, completely cuts through conceit, and puts an end to suffering.'

A monk who has seen the pleasant as
painful, the painful as an arrow, and
the peacefulness that is neither pleas-
ant nor painful as impermanent,

Adukkhamasukhaṃ santaṃ, addakkhi
nаṃ aniccato
Sa ve sammaddaso bhikkhu, parijānāti
vedanā.

So vedanā pariññāya, diṭṭhe dhamme
anāsavo;
Kāyassa bhedā dhammaṭṭho, saṅkhyaṃ
nopeti vedagū ti.

Sallasuttaṃ

Assutavā, bhikkhave, puthujjano sukhampi vedanaṃ vedayati, dukkhampi vedanaṃ vedayati, adukkhamasukhampi vedanaṃ vedayati. Sutavā, bhikkhave, ariyasāvako sukhampi vedanaṃ vedayati, dukkhampi vedanaṃ vedayati, adukkhamasukhampi vedanaṃ vedayati. Tatra, bhikkhave, ko viseso ko adhippayāso kiṃ nānākaraṇaṃ sutavato ariyasāvakassa assutavatā puthujjanenā ti?

sees correctly and thoroughly under-
stands feelings.
One thoroughly understanding feelings
is free of destructive predispositions
in this life;
and when the body gives way, one
grounded in truth possesses a
knowledge that cannot be
calculated."

The Arrow

"Monks, an uninformed ordinary person feels a pleasant feeling, a painful feeling, and a neutral feeling. And the well-informed noble disciple feels a pleasant feeling, a painful feeling, and a neutral feeling. What is the distinction here, monks? What is the particular point? What is the difference between the well-informed noble disciple and the uninformed ordinary person?"

Bhagavaṃmūlakā no, bhante, dhammā, bhagavaṃnettikā, bhagavaṃpaṭisaraṇā. Sādhu vata, bhante, bhagavantaṃyeva paṭibhātu etassa bhāsitassa attho. Bhagavato sutvā bhikkhū dhāressantī ti.*

Bhikkhave, puthujjano dukkhāya vedanāya phuṭṭho samāno socati kilamati paridevati urattāḷiṃ kandati sammohaṃ āpajjati. So dve vedanā vedayati—kāyikañca, cetasikañca.

Seyyathāpi, bhikkhave, purisaṃ sallena vijjheyya. Tamenaṃ dutiyena sallena anuvedhaṃ vijjheyya. Evañhi so, bhikkhave, puriso dvisallena vedanaṃ vedayati. Evameva kho, bhikkhave, assutavā puthujjano dukkhāya vedanāya phuṭṭho samāno socati kilamati

* I have added the full sentence (repeated earlier in the text) for the abbreviated version here which is: Bhagavaṃmūlakā no, bhante, dhammā . . . pe . . . assutavā.

"Sir, our teachings are rooted in the Buddha, guided by the Buddha, protected by the Buddha. It would be good, sir, for the Buddha to make clear the meaning of what has been said. Hearing the Buddha, the monks will remember it."

"Monks, an ordinary person who is being affected by a painful feeling grieves, gets exhausted, weeps, beats their breast, and becomes unhinged. One feels two feelings—bodily and mental.

"Monks, suppose one were to pierce a man with an arrow, and then pierce him immediately after with a second arrow, so that the man would experience a feeling caused by two arrows. It is like this, monks, for the uninformed ordinary person who, being affected by a painful feeling, grieves, gets exhausted, weeps, beats his breast, and becomes unhinged. He feels two feelings—bodily and mental.

paridevati urattāḷiṃ kandati sammohaṃ āpajjati. So dve vedanā vedayati—kāyikañca, cetasikañca.

Tassāyeva kho pana dukkhāya vedanāya phuṭṭho samāno paṭighavā hoti. Tamenaṃ dukkhāya vedanāya paṭighavantaṃ, yo dukkhāya vedanāya paṭighānusayo, so anuseti. So dukkhāya vedanāya phuṭṭho samāno kāmasukhaṃ abhinandati. Taṃ kissa hetu? Na hi so, bhikkhave, pajānāti assutavā puthujjano aññatra kāmasukhā dukkhāya vedanāya nissaraṇaṃ, tassa kāmasukhañca abhinandato, yo sukhāya vedanāya rāgānusayo, so anuseti. So tāsaṃ vedanānaṃ samudayañca atthaṅgamañca assādañca ādīnavañca nissaraṇañca yathābhūtaṃ nappajānāti. Tassa tāsaṃ vedanānaṃ samudayañca atthaṅgamañca assādañca ādīnavañca nissaraṇañca yathābhūtaṃ appajānato, yo adukkhamasukhāya vedanāya avijjānusayo, so anuseti.

"But now suppose that while he is being affected by the painful feeling he has an aversion toward it. When he has aversion toward that painful feeling, the underlying tendency of aversion toward painful feelings is present below the surface. And while being affected with a painful feeling, he welcomes sensual pleasures. Why is this? It is because the uninformed ordinary person does not know any escape from painful feelings other than sensual pleasures. And when he welcomes sensual pleasures, the underlying tendency of desire for pleasant feeling is present below the surface. He does not truly understand the rising and passing away of feelings, their gratification and downside, and their escape. And when one

So sukhañce vedanaṃ vedayati, saññutto naṃ vedayati. Dukkhañce vedanaṃ vedayati, saññutto naṃ vedayati. Adukkhamasukhañce vedanaṃ vedayati, saññutto naṃ vedayati. Ayaṃ vuccati, bhikkhave, assutavā puthujjano saññutto jātiyā jarāya maraṇena sokehi paridevehi dukkhehi domanassehi upāyāsehi, saññutto dukkhasmāti vadāmi.

Sutavā ca kho, bhikkhave, ariyasāvako dukkhāya vedanāya phuṭṭho samāno na socati, na kilamati, na paridevati, na urattāḷiṃ kandati, na sammohaṃ āpajjati. So ekaṃ vedanaṃ vedayati—kāyikaṃ, na cetasikaṃ.

is not truly understanding the rising and passing away of feelings, their gratification and downside, and their escape, the underlying tendency of ignorance toward a neutral feeling is present below the surface.

"When he feels a pleasant feeling, he feels it with attachment. When he feels a painful feeling, he feels it with attachment. And when he feels a neutral feeling, he feels it with attachment. I say that this refers to how the uninformed ordinary person is attached to birth, old age, and death, attached to grief and weeping, attached to pain, distress, and trouble, and attached to suffering.

"On the other hand, monks, a well-informed noble disciple when being affected by painful feeling does not grieve, get exhausted, weep, beat their breast, or become unhinged. One feels one feeling—the bodily, but not the mental.

Seyyathāpi, bhikkhave, purisaṃ sallena vijjheyya. Tamenaṃ dutiyena sallena anuvedhaṃ na vijjheyya. Evañhi so, bhikkhave, puriso ekasallena vedanaṃ vedayati. Evameva kho, bhikkhave, sutavā ariyasāvako dukkhāya vedanāya phuṭṭho samāno na socati, na kilamati, na paridevati, na urattāḷiṃ kandati, na sammohaṃ āpajjati. So ekaṃ vedanaṃ vedayati—kāyikaṃ, na cetasikaṃ.

Tassāyeva kho pana dukkhāya vedanāya phuṭṭho samāno paṭighavā na hoti. Tamenaṃ dukkhāya vedanāya appaṭighavantaṃ, yo dukkhāya vedanāya paṭighānusayo, so nānuseti. So dukkhāya vedanāya phuṭṭho samāno kāmasukhaṃ nābhinandati. Taṃ kissa hetu? Pajānāti hi so, bhikkhave, sutavā ariyasāvako aññatra kāmasukhā dukkhāya vedanāya nissaraṇaṃ. Tassa kāmasukhaṃ nābhinandato yo sukhāya vedanāya rāgānusayo, so

"Again, suppose one were to pierce a man with an arrow, but not pierce him with a second arrow, so that the man would experience a feeling caused by just one arrow. It is like this, monks, for the informed noble disciple who is affected by a painful feeling but does not grieve, get exhausted, weep, beat his breast, or become unhinged. He feels one feeling—the bodily, but not the mental.

"And now suppose that while he is being affected by the painful feeling he does not have an aversion toward it. Not having an aversion toward the painful feeling, no underlying tendency of aversion toward painful feeling is present below the surface. And while being affected with painful feeling, he does not welcome sensual pleasures. Why is this? It is because the well-informed noble disciple knows that there is an escape

nānuseti. So tāsaṃ vedanānaṃ samudayañca atthaṅgamañca assādañca ādīnavaṃ ca nissaraṇañca yathābhūtaṃ pajānāti. Tassa tāsaṃ vedanānaṃ samudayañca atthaṅgamañca assādañca ādīnavañca nissaraṇañca yathābhūtaṃ pajānato, yo adukkhamasukhāya vedanāya avijjānusayo, so nānuseti.

So sukhañce vedanaṃ vedayati, visaññutto naṃ vedayati. Dukkhañce vedanaṃ vedayati, visaññutto naṃ vedayati. Adukkhamasukhañce vedanaṃ vedayati, visaññutto naṃ vedayati. Ayaṃ vuccati, bhikkhave, 'sutavā ariyasāvako visaññutto jātiyā jarāya maraṇena sokehi paridevehi dukkhehi domanassehi upāyāsehi, visaññutto dukkhasmā'ti vadāmi.

from painful feeling other than sensual pleasures. And when he does not welcome sensual pleasures, no underlying tendency of desire for pleasant feeling is present below the surface. He truly understands feelings' arising and passing away, their gratification and downside, and their escape. And when one who truly understands feelings' arising and passing away, their gratification and downside, and their escape, no underlying tendency of ignorance toward a neutral feeling is present below the surface.

"When he feels a pleasant feeling, he feels it without attachment. And when he feels a painful feeling, he feels it without attachment. And when he feels a neutral feeling, he feels it without attachment. I say that this refers to how the informed noble disciple is not attached to birth, old age, and death, not attached to grief and weeping, not attached

Ayaṃ kho, bhikkhave, viseso, ayaṃ adhippayāso, idaṃ nānākaraṇaṃ sutavato ariyasāvakassa assutavatā puthujjanenā"ti.

Na vedanaṃ vedayati sapañño,
Sukhampi dukkhampi bahussutopi;
Ayañca dhīrassa puthujjanena,
Mahāviseso kusalassa hoti.

Saṅkhātadhammassa bahussutassa,
Vipassato lokamimaṃ parañca;
Iṭṭhassa dhammā na mathenti cittaṃ,
Aniṭṭhato no paṭighātameti.

to pain, distress, and trouble, and not attached to suffering.

"This, monks, is the distinction, the particular point, and the difference between the well-informed noble disciple and the uninformed ordinary person.

One with wisdom and learning does not
feel feeling as either pleasant or
painful.
The good make this huge distinction
between the wise and the ordinary
person.
The learned one who has comprehended
the truth and has insight into this
world and the next
does not let agreeable things agitate the
mind and is not repelled by what is
disagreeable.

Tassānurodhā athavā virodhā,
Vidhūpitā atthagatā na santi;
Padañca ñatvā virajaṃ asoka
Sammā pajānāti bhavassa pāragū ti.

One's liking and disliking are no more,
scattered and annihilated.
Knowing the dustless and sorrowless
way,
one who has crossed over truly
understands."

■ ■ ■

The next teaching addresses anyone in acute or chronic pain. It describes the Buddha working with monks who are in hospital or hospice, facing pain and death. It mentions the four applications of mindfulness—watching body in body, feeling in feeling, mind in mind, and phenomena in phenomena. One attends to the pain closely, observing and registering what one experiences, and then comes to see that it is conditioned and dependent on the body, which in turn is also conditioned and dependent on other phenomena. As conditioned and dependent, feeling, body, and all phenomena are transient—they will dissolve and fade away.

The notion of "condition" in Buddhism refers to circumstances that are necessary for something to occur, even if they are not a direct or immediate cause. The standard formulation is "if x, then y," where condition x may or may not be a direct cause of event y, but in its absence "y" would not occur. The wick and the oil in an oil lamp are some of the conditions for a flame, and without them the flame goes out.

The purpose of attending to the manifold conditions of an experience is to come to see that they too rely on further conditions. When everything is dependent on conditions, nothing is permanent, essential, or isolated in itself.

Modern mental health programs utilizing this kind of meditation practice have increasingly become a helpful tool for pain management. There is considerable evidence that turning toward the pain and its conditions with curiosity and equanimity can help the mind disengage from them and bring genuine and sustained relief.[2]

Paṭhamagelaññasuttaṃ

Ekaṃ samayaṃ bhagavā vesāliyaṃ viharati mahāvane kūṭāgārasālāyaṃ. Atha kho bhagavā sāyanhasamayaṃ paṭisallānā vuṭṭhito yena gilānasālā tenupasaṅkami; upasaṅkamitvā paññatte āsane nisīdi. Nisajja kho bhagavā bhikkhū āmantesi—

Sato, bhikkhave, bhikkhu sampajāno kālaṃ āgameyya. Ayaṃ vo amhākaṃ anusāsanī.

Kathañca, bhikkhave, bhikkhu sato hoti? Idha, bhikkhave, bhikkhu kāye kāyānupassī viharati ātāpī sampajāno satimā, vineyya loke abhijjhādomanassaṃ; vedanāsu vedanānupassī viharati . . . pe . . . citte cittānupassī viharati . . . pe . . . dhammesu dhammānupassī viharati ātāpī sampajāno satimā, vineyya loke abhijjhādomanassaṃ. Evaṃ kho, bhikkhave, bhikkhu sato hoti.

Illness

At one time the Buddha was staying in the Great Wood at Vesali, in the Hall with the Peaked Roof. In the evening the Buddha emerged from seclusion and went to the sick ward where he sat on his appointed seat. Once seated, he addressed the monks:

"Monks, a monk approaching the hour of death should be mindful and clearly comprehending. This is my teaching to you.

"Monks, how is a monk mindful? Here a monk lives, watching the body in the body, energetic, clearly comprehending, mindful, letting go of both longing for the world and depression. One lives watching feelings in feelings . . . lives watching mind in mind . . . and lives watching phenomena in phenomena, energetic, clearly comprehending, mindful, letting go of both longing for the world and depression. In this way, monks, a monk is mindful.

Kathañca, bhikkhave, bhikkhu sampajāno hoti? Idha, bhikkhave, bhikkhu abhikkante paṭikkante sampajānakārī hoti, ālokite vilokite sampajānakārī hoti, samiñjite pasārite sampajānakārī hoti, saṅghāṭipattacīvaradhāraṇe sampajānakārī hoti, asite pīte khāyite sāyite sampajānakārī hoti, uccārapassāvakamme sampajānakārī hoti, gate ṭhite nisinne sutte jāgarite bhāsite tuṇhībhāve sampajānakārī hoti. Evaṃ kho, bhikkhave, bhikkhu sampajānakārī hoti. Sato, bhikkhave, bhikkhu sampajāno kālaṃ āgameyya. Ayaṃ vo amhākaṃ anusāsanī.

Tassa ce, bhikkhave, bhikkhuno evaṃ satassa sampajānassa appamattassa ātāpino pahitattassa viharato uppajjati sukhā vedanā, so evaṃ pajānāti—uppannā kho me ayaṃ sukhā

"And how, monks, is a monk clearly comprehending? Here a monk is fully attentive whether approaching or retreating, whether looking forward or looking back, and whether bending or stretching. One is fully attentive while wearing the robe and carrying one's outer robe and alms bowl, and while eating, drinking, chewing food, and tasting it. One is fully attentive while answering the calls of nature and while moving, standing, sitting, going to sleep, waking, speaking, and remaining silent. In this way, monks, a monk is clearly comprehending. Monks, a monk approaching death should be mindful and clearly comprehending. This is my teaching to you.

"When a pleasant feeling occurs for a monk spending their time mindfully, clearly comprehending, and with care, effort, and determination, they understand it in this

vedanā. Sā ca kho paṭicca, no appaṭicca. Kiṃ paṭicca? Imameva kāyaṃ paṭicca. Ayaṃ kho pana kāyo anicco saṅkhato paṭiccasamuppanno. Aniccaṃ kho pana saṅkhataṃ paṭiccasamuppannaṃ kāyaṃ paṭicca uppannā sukhā vedanā kuto niccā bhavissatīti! So kāye ca sukhāya ca vedanāya aniccānupassī viharati, vayānupassī viharati, virāgānupassī viharati, nirodhānupassī viharati, paṭinissaggānupassī viharati. Tassa kāye ca sukhāya ca vedanāya aniccānupassino viharato, vayānupassino viharato, virāgānupassino viharato, nirodhānupassino viharato, paṭinissaggānupassino viharato, yo kāye ca sukhāya ca vedanāya rāgānusayo, so pahīyati.

way: *A pleasant feeling has occurred in me. It has a condition; it is not without conditions. What is its condition? Its condition is just this body. But the body is impermanent, itself produced by a combination of conditions, and dependently arisen. How could a pleasant feeling that occurs dependent on a body that is impermanent, produced by a combination of conditions, and dependently arisen, be permanent?* So, they spend their time watching the impermanence in the body and in pleasant feelings, watching their deterioration, watching their fading away, watching their stopping, and watching their dropping off. And one who spends their time watching the impermanence in the body and in pleasant feelings, watching their deterioration, fading away, stopping, and dropping off, lets go of the underlying

Tassa ce, bhikkhave, bhikkhuno evaṃ satassa sampajānassa appamattassa ātāpino pahitattassa viharato uppajjati dukkhā vedanā. So evaṃ pajānāti—uppannā kho myāyaṃ dukkhā vedanā. Sā ca kho paṭicca, no appaṭicca. Kiṃ paṭicca? Imameva kāyaṃ paṭicca. Ayaṃ kho pana kāyo anicco saṅkhato paṭiccasamuppanno. Aniccaṃ kho pana saṅkhataṃ paṭiccasamuppannaṃ kāyaṃ paṭicca uppannā dukkhā vedanā kuto niccā bhavissatī'ti! So kāye ca dukkhāya vedanāya aniccānupassī viharati, vayānupassī viharati, virāgānupassī viharati, nirodhānupassī viharati, paṭinissaggānupassī viharati. Tassa kāye ca dukkhāya ca vedanāya aniccānupassino viharato . . . pe . . . paṭinissaggānupassino viharato, yo kāye ca dukkhāya ca vedanāya paṭighānusayo, so pahīyati.

tendency of desire for the body and pleasant feelings.

"When a painful feeling occurs for a monk spending their time mindfully, clearly comprehending, and with care, effort, and determination, they understand it in this way: *A painful feeling has occurred in me. It has a condition; it is not without conditions. What is its condition? Its condition is just this body. But the body is impermanent, itself produced by a combination of conditions, and dependently arisen. How could a painful feeling that occurs dependent on a body that is impermanent, produced by a combination of conditions, and dependently arisen, be permanent?* So, they spend their time watching the impermanence in the body and in painful feelings, watching their deterioration, watching their fading away, watching their stopping, and watching their dropping off. And

Tassa ce, bhikkhave, bhikkhuno evaṃ satassa sampajānassa appamattassa ātāpino pahitattassa viharato uppajjati adukkhamasukhā vedanā, so evaṃ pajānāti—'uppannā kho myāyaṃ adukkhamasukhā vedanā. Sā ca kho paṭicca, no appaṭicca. Kiṃ paṭicca? Imameva kāyaṃ paṭicca. Ayaṃ kho pana kāyo anicco saṅkhato paṭiccasamuppanno. Aniccaṃ kho pana saṅkhataṃ paṭiccasamuppannaṃ kāyaṃ paṭicca uppannā adukkhamasukhā vedanā kuto niccā bhavissatīti! So kāye ca adukkhamasukhāya ca vedanāya aniccānupassī viharati, vayānupassī viharati, virāgānupassī

one who spends their time watching the impermanence in the body and in painful feelings, watching their deterioration, fading away, stopping, and dropping off, lets go of the underlying tendency of aversion toward the body and painful feelings.

"When a neutral feeling occurs for a monk spending their time mindfully, clearly comprehending, and with care, effort, and determination, they understand it in this way: *A neutral feeling has occurred in me. It has a condition; it is not without conditions. What is its condition? Its condition is just this body. But the body is impermanent, itself produced by a combination of conditions, and dependently arisen. How could a neutral feeling that occurs dependent on a body that is impermanent, produced by a combination of conditions, and dependently*

viharati, nirodhānupassī viharati, paṭinissaggānupassī viharati. Tassa kāye ca adukkhamasukhāya ca vedanāya aniccānupassino viharato . . . pe . . . paṭinissaggānupassino viharato, yo kāye ca adukkhamasukhāya ca vedanāya avijjānusayo, so pahīyati.

So sukhañce vedanaṃ vedayati, sā aniccāti pajānāti, anajjhositāti pajānāti, anabhinanditāti pajānāti; dukkhañce vedanaṃ vedayati, sā aniccāti pajānāti, anajjhositāti pajānāti, anabhinanditāti pajānāti; adukkhamasukhañce vedanaṃ vedayati, sā aniccāti pajānāti, anajjhositāti pajānāti, anabhinanditāti pajānāti.

arisen, be permanent? So, they live watching the impermanence in the body and in neutral feelings, watching their deterioration, watching their fading away, watching their stopping, and watching their dropping off. And one who spends their time watching their impermanence, dropping off, and so on, lets go of the underlying tendency of ignorance toward the body and neutral feelings.

"One feels a pleasant feeling and understands: *This is impermanent.* One understands: *This is not held on to.* One understands: *This is not delighted in.* One feels a painful feeling and understands: *This is impermanent.* One understands: *This is not held on to.* One understands: *This is not delighted in.* One feels a neutral feeling and understands: *This is impermanent.* One understands: *This is*

So sukhañce vedanaṃ vedayati, visaññutto naṃ vedayati; dukkhañce vedanaṃ vedayati, visaññutto naṃ vedayati; adukkhamasukhañce vedanaṃ vedayati, visaññutto naṃ vedayati. So kāyapariyantikaṃ vedanaṃ vedayamāno kāyapariyantikaṃ vedanaṃ vedayāmīti pajānāti, jīvitapariyantikaṃ vedanaṃ vedayamāno jīvitapariyantikaṃ vedanaṃ vedayāmīti pajānāti. Kāyassa bhedā uddhaṃ jīvitapariyādānā idheva sabbavedayitāni anabhinanditāni sītibhavissantīti pajānāti.

Seyyathāpi, bhikkhave, telañca paṭicca vaṭṭiñca paṭicca telappadīpo jhāyeyya, tasseva telassa ca vaṭṭiyā ca pariyādānā anāhāro nibbāyeyya; evameva kho, bhikkhave, bhikkhu

not held on to. One understands: *This is not delighted in.*

"One feels a pleasant feeling and feels it with detachment. One feels a painful feeling and feels it with detachment. One feels a neutral feeling and feels it with detachment. Feeling a feeling that is ending with the body, one understands: *I am feeling a feeling ending with the body.* Feeling a feeling ending with life, one understands: *I am feeling a feeling ending with life.* And so, one understands: *In time, when the body gives way at the end of life, everything that is felt here cannot be delighted in and will become cool.*

"Monks, just as an oil lamp that burns dependent on the oil and dependent on the wick is extinguished at the end of the oil and the wick due to lack of fuel, so too a

kāyapariyantikaṃ vedanaṃ vedayamāno kāyapariyantikaṃ vedanaṃ vedayāmīti pajānāti. Jīvitapariyantikaṃ vedanaṃ vedayamāno jīvitapariyantikaṃ vedanaṃ vedayāmīti pajānāti. Kāyassa bhedā uddhaṃ jīvitapariyādānā idheva sabbavedayitāni anabhinanditāni sītībhavissantīti pajānātīti.

monk feeling a feeling that is ending with the body understands: *I am feeling a feeling ending with the body*. And one feeling a feeling ending with life understands: *I am feeling a feeling ending with life.* One understands: *In time, when the body gives way at the end of life, everything that is felt here cannot be delighted in and will become cool.*"

▪▪▪

The Buddha once declared that it is impossible to fully isolate feelings from perceptions and consciousness; given how entangled they are, we only ever experience them jumbled together and interacting.[3] *What he does offer is analytic distinctions that help us begin to track these phenomena to spot the conditions for them.*

The next two passages begin to dig into how feelings are constructed and dependent on other conditions. And it is precisely because of their being dependent on conditions, what the texts call "dependently arisen," that they can be tackled.

So what, most immediately, precedes and stimulates feelings?

One important analysis is in our second passage focusing on sensory contact. When we notice how our senses are making contact with their objects we can exert some measure of control over feelings. It is by disengaging from the sensory contact that typically immediately precedes them that feelings can be calmed. This approach is part of the rationale for the monastic life insofar as its austerities remove many of the kinds of sensory contact and objects that distract, trouble, or enchant us. While the Buddha rejected ex-

treme asceticism, his monks live celibate lives that also limit food intake and creature comforts. They are thus, at least in principle, free from the trappings and hustle of life in the world.

Aniccasuttaṃ

Tisso imā, bhikkhave, vedanā aniccā saṅkhatā paṭiccasamuppannā khayadhammā vayadhammā virāgadhammā nirodhadhammā. Katamā tisso? Sukhā vedanā, dukkhā vedanā, adukkhamasukhā vedanā—imā kho, bhikkhave, tisso vedanā aniccā saṅkhatā paṭiccasamuppannā khayadhammā vayadhammā virāgadhammā nirodhadhammāti.

Phassamūlakasuttaṃ

Tisso imā, bhikkhave, vedanā phassajā phassamūlakā phassanidānā phassapaccayā. Katamā tisso? Sukhā vedanā, dukkhā vedanā, adukkhamasukhā vedanā. Sukhavedaniyaṃ, bhikkhave, phassaṃ paṭicca uppajjati sukhā vedanā. Tasseva sukhavedaniyassa phassassa nirodhā, yaṃ tajjaṃ vedayitaṃ sukhavedaniyaṃ phassaṃ paṭicca uppannā sukhā vedanā,

Impermanence

"Monks, there are three kinds of feelings that are impermanent, constructed, and dependently arisen. They can be lost, they can fade away, and they can cease. What are the three? Pleasant feeling, painful feeling, and neutral feeling. Monks, these three feelings are impermanent, constructed, and dependently arisen. They disappear, they deteriorate, they fade away, and they cease."

Rooted in Sensory Contact

"Monks, there are three kinds of feelings born of sensory contact, rooted in sensory contact, having their origin in sensory contact, and dependent on sensory contact. What are the three? Pleasant feeling, painful feeling, and neutral feeling. Pleasant feeling occurs dependent on agreeable sensory contact. When the agreeable sensory contact

sā nirujjhati, sā vūpasammati. Dukkhavedaniyaṃ, bhikkhave, phassaṃ paṭicca uppajjati dukkhā vedanā. Tasseva dukkhavedaniyassa phassassa nirodhā, yaṃ tajjaṃ vedayitaṃ dukkhavedaniyaṃ phassaṃ paṭicca uppannā dukkhā vedanā, sā nirujjhati, sā vūpasammati. Adukkhamasukhavedaniyaṃ, bhikkhave, phassaṃ paṭicca uppajjati adukkhamasukhā vedanā. Tasseva adukkhamasukhavedaniyassa phassassa nirodhā, yaṃ tajjaṃ vedayitaṃ adukkhamasukhavedaniyaṃ phassaṃ paṭicca uppannā adukkhamasukhā vedanā, sā nirujjhati, sā vūpasammati.

Seyyathāpi, bhikkhave, dvinnaṃ kaṭṭhānaṃ saṅghaṭṭanasamodhānā usmā jāyati, tejo abhinibbattati. Tesaṃyeva kaṭṭhānaṃ nānābhāvā vinikkhepā, yā tajjā usmā, sā nirujjhati, sā vūpasammati. Evameva kho, bhikkhave, imā tisso vedanā phassajā phas-

stops, the pleasant feeling that occurs dependent on the corresponding agreeable sensory contact ceases and is extinguished. Painful feeling occurs dependent on disagreeable sensory contact. When that disagreeable sensory contact stops, the painful feeling that occurs dependent on the corresponding disagreeable sensory contact ceases and is extinguished. Neutral feeling occurs dependent on neutral sensory contact. When that neutral sensory contact stops, the neutral feeling that occurs dependent on the corresponding neutral sensory contact ceases and is extinguished.

"Monks, when two sticks are rubbed together, they generate heat and produce fire. But when the sticks are separated and held apart, the corresponding heat ceases and is extinguished. So too, monks, these three feelings are born of sensory contact, rooted

samūlakā phassanidānā phassapaccayā. Tajjaṃ phassaṃ paṭicca tajjā vedanā uppajjanti. Tajjassa phassassa nirodhā tajjā vedanā nirujjhantīti.

in sensory contact, having their origin in sensory contact, and dependent on sensory contact. Feelings are produced dependent on their corresponding sensory contact. Stopping their corresponding sensory contact, feelings cease."

■ ■ ■

The logic of Buddhist treatments of experience rests on the insight that even conditions are conditioned by conditions. If sensory contact immediately prompts feeling, then what prompts sensory contact? While we need not go into depth exploring all of the conditioning factors underlying all psychological states, one of the most important conditions shaping sensory contact is what the Buddhists call "habitual patterns."

Habitual patterns are the predispositions and inclinations, based on past experiences, that help determine what we become conscious of in the first place. For example, if I am habituated (by past experience, temperament, social conditioning, being hungry, etc.) to being particularly drawn to food on certain occasions, I may become aware of the dinner on the table before or instead of noticing friends and colleagues sitting around it, the warmth of the room, or the color of the wallpaper. Other guests at the same event might become aware of different features of this experience based on their preexisting biases and habitual patterns. Our senses make contact with what we are already preconditioned to notice, and our feelings follow.

The next passage suggests that conditioned by the partial and biased nature of our habitual patterns, we are predisposed to finding even pleasant and neutral feelings painful.

This idea repeats a theme we've been exploring, but more precisely locates the dissatisfaction in all feeling as a function of these biased preconditions. The text then goes on to explore a kind of pleasure or happiness that is not conditioned by such habitual patterns.

In this vein, the Buddha is represented in the early discourses as subverting ordinary ideas about sukha and dukkha:

> *What others speak of as pleasure, the*
> *noble ones speak of as pain.*
> *What others speak of as pain, the noble*
> *ones know as pleasure.*[4]

This is to say that ordinary people tend to think that sensory pleasure is pleasant or brings happiness. But the Buddha's monastic disciples—the "noble ones"—spot the transience and ultimately frustrating nature of even pleasant sensations, and so see them entailing a kind of suffering or pain.

And while ordinary people might think that the monastic life taught by the Buddha—austere, simplified, celibate—is painful or causes suffering, his disciples know that it contains the pleasure and happiness of states of meditation that transcend sensory experience.

The passage suggests both of these teachings: first, that anything felt by the senses is painful in a certain sense, and second, that a monk developing the mind through meditation comes to feel rarified experiences of pleasure that are not based on sensory contact. The first four levels of advanced meditation are called "meditative absorptions." They result from gradually disengaging from the senses and thereby reaching higher and more refined depths of focus. Beyond that, the mind enters "dimensions," or spheres of awareness (or, perhaps, "flow states") that are not restricted by our usual notions of space, consciousness, existence, and perception.[5] *These highly elevated modes of awareness are ways of experiencing sublime pleasure that have nothing to do with sensory pleasure or worldly desire.*

Rahogatasuttaṃ

Atha kho aññataro bhikkhu yena bhagavā tenupasaṅkami; upasaṅkamitvā bhagavantaṃ abhivādetvā ekamantaṃ nisīdi. Ekamantaṃ nisinno kho so bhikkhu bhagavantaṃ etadavoca—idha mayhaṃ, bhante, rahogatassa paṭisallīnassa evaṃ cetaso parivitakko udapādi—tisso vedanā vuttā bhagavatā. Sukhā vedanā, dukkhā vedanā, adukkhamasukhā vedanā—imā tisso vedanā vuttā bhagavatā. Vuttaṃ kho panetaṃ bhagavatā—yaṃ kiñci vedayitaṃ taṃ dukkhasminti. Kiṃ nu kho etaṃ bhagavatā sandhāya bhāsitaṃ—yaṃ kiñci vedayitaṃ taṃ dukkhasminti?

Sādhu sādhu, bhikkhu! Tisso imā, bhikkhu, vedanā vuttā mayā. Sukhā vedanā, dukkhā vedanā, adukkhamasukhā vedanā—imā tisso vedanā vuttā mayā. Vuttaṃ kho panetaṃ, bhikkhu, mayā—yaṃ kiñci vedayitaṃ, taṃ dukkhasminti. Taṃ kho panetaṃ, bhikkhu,

Being Alone

Now, a certain monk approached the Buddha, greeted him cordially, and sat down to one side. Sitting to the side, the monk spoke to the Buddha: "Sir, when I was alone and practicing solitude here, I had this train of thought: *Three kinds of feelings are mentioned by the Buddha. The three kinds of feelings mentioned by the Buddha are pleasant feeling, painful feeling, and neutral feeling. However, the Buddha also said: 'Anything felt is included in the painful.'* What was the Buddha referring to when he said, 'Anything felt is included in the painful'?"

"Well done, monk, well done! I have mentioned these three kinds of feelings. The three kinds of feelings mentioned by me are pleasant feeling, painful feeling, and neutral feeling. I also said that 'Anything felt is in-

mayā saṅkhārānaṃyeva aniccataṃ sandhāya bhāsitaṃ—yaṃ kiñci vedayitaṃ taṃ dukkhasminti. Taṃ kho panetaṃ, bhikkhu, mayā saṅkhārānaṃyeva khayadhammataṃ . . . pe . . . vayadhammataṃ . . . pe . . . virāgadhammataṃ . . . pe . . . nirodhadhammataṃ . . . pe . . . vipariṇāmadhammataṃ sandhāya bhāsitaṃ—yaṃ kiñci vedayitaṃ taṃ dukkhasminti.

Atha kho pana, bhikkhu, mayā anupubbasaṅkhārānaṃ nirodho akkhāto. Paṭhamaṃ jhānaṃ samāpannassa vācā niruddhā hoti. Dutiyaṃ jhānaṃ samāpannassa vitakkavicārā niruddhā honti. Tatiyaṃ jhānaṃ samāpannassa pīti niruddhā hoti. Catutthaṃ jhānaṃ samāpannassa assāsapassāsā niruddhā honti. Ākāsānañcāyatanaṃ samāpannassa rūpasaññā niruddhā hoti. Viññāṇañcāyatanaṃ samāpannassa ākāsānañcāyatanasaññā nirud-

cluded in the painful.' But I said this in reference to the impermanence of the habitual patterns, and so I said that 'Anything felt is included in the painful.' Indeed, I have said in reference to the habitual patterns that they disappear, deteriorate, fade away, and cease, and in that sense anything felt is included in the painful.

"But, monk, I have also described the gradual ceasing of the habitual patterns. For one who has reached the first meditative absorption, speech ceases. For one who has reached the second meditative absorption, thought and deliberation cease. For one who has reached the third meditative absorption, joy ceases. For one who has reached the fourth meditative absorption, labored breathing in and out ceases.[6] For one who has reached the dimension of infinite space,

dhā hoti. Ākiñcaññāyatanaṃ samāpannassa viññāṇañcāyatanasaññā niruddhā hoti. Nevasaññānāsaññāyatanaṃ samāpannassa ākiñcaññāyatanasaññā niruddhā hoti. Saññāvedayitanirodhaṃ samāpannassa saññā ca vedanā ca niruddhā honti. Khīṇāsavassa bhikkhuno rāgo niruddho hoti, doso niruddho hoti, moho niruddho hoti.

Atha kho, bhikkhu, mayā anupubbasaṅkhārānaṃ vūpasamo akkhāto. Paṭhamaṃ jhānaṃ samāpannassa vācā vūpasantā hoti. Dutiyaṃ jhānaṃ samāpannassa vitakkavicārā vūpasantā honti . . . pe . . . saññāvedayitan-

the perception of material objects ceases. For one who has reached the dimension of infinite consciousness, the perception of the dimension of infinite space ceases. For one who has reached the dimension of nothingness, the perception of infinite consciousness ceases. For one who has reached the dimension of neither perception nor nonperception, the dimension of nothingness ceases. For one who has reached the cessation of perception and feeling, perception and feeling cease. For the awakened monk, desire has ceased, hatred has ceased, and delusion has ceased.

"I have also described, monk, the gradual calming of the habitual patterns. For one who has reached the first meditative absorption, speech is calmed. For one who has reached the second meditative absorption,

irodhaṃ samāpannassa saññā ca vedanā ca vūpasantā honti. Khīṇāsavassa bhikkhuno rāgo vūpasanto hoti, doso vūpasanto hoti, moho vūpasanto hoti.

Chayimā, bhikkhu, passaddhiyo. Paṭhamaṃ jhānaṃ samāpannassa vācā paṭippassaddhā hoti. Dutiyaṃ jhānaṃ samāpannassa vitakkavicārā paṭippassaddhā honti. Tatiyaṃ jhānaṃ samāpannassa pīti paṭippassaddhā hoti. Catutthaṃ jhānaṃ samāpannassa assāsapassāsā paṭippassaddhā honti. Saññāvedayitanirodhaṃ samāpannassa saññā ca vedanā ca paṭippassaddhā honti. Khīṇāsavassa bhikkhuno rāgo paṭippassaddho hoti, doso paṭippassaddho hoti, moho paṭippassaddho hotīti.

thought, and deliberation are calmed . . . And so on up through the one who has reached the cessation of perception and feeling, for whom perception and feeling are calmed. For the awakened monk, desire is calmed, hatred is calmed, and delusion is calmed.

"Monk, there are six kinds of serenity. For one who has reached the first meditative absorption, speech is quieted. For one who has reached the second meditative absorption, thought and deliberation are quieted. For one who has reached the third meditative absorption, joy is quieted. For one who has reached the fourth meditative absorption, labored breathing in and out is quieted. For the one who has reached the cessation of perception and feeling, perception and feeling are quieted. For the awakened monk,

Paṭhamākāsasuttaṃ

Seyyathāpi, bhikkhave, ākāse vividhā vātā vāyanti. Puratthimāpi vātā vāyanti, pacchimāpi vātā vāyanti, uttarāpi vātā vāyanti, dakkhiṇāpi vātā vāyanti, sarajāpi vātā vāyanti, arajāpi vātā vāyanti, sītāpi vātā vāyanti, uṇhāpi vātā vāyanti, parittāpi vātā vāyanti, adhimattāpi vātā vāyanti. Evameva kho, bhikkhave, imasmiṃ kāyasmiṃ vividhā vedanā uppajjanti, sukhāpi vedanā uppajjati, dukkhāpi vedanā uppajjati, adukkhamasukhāpi vedanā uppajjatīti.

desire is quieted, hatred is quieted, and delusion is quieted."

■ ■ ■

To encourage people to disengage from the feelings and emotions that can take us over, the Buddha urges that one see their ephemerality. They come and they go like winds in the sky and guests in a guesthouse.

The Sky

"Consider, monks, how various winds blow through the sky: winds from the east blow, winds from the west blow, winds from the north blow, and winds from the south blow; dusty winds blow and dustless winds blow; cold winds blow and hot winds blow; small breezes blow and great gales blow. Similarly, monks, various feelings arise in this body: pleasant feelings arise, painful feelings arise, and neutral feelings arise.

Yathāpi vātā ākāse, vāyanti vividhā puthū;
Puratthimā pacchimā cāpi, uttarā atha
dakkhiṇā.
Sarajā arajā capi, sītā uṇhā ca ekadā;
Adhimattā parittā ca, puthū vāyanti
mālutā.

Tathevimasmiṃ kāyasmiṃ, samuppajjanti
vedanā;
Sukhadukkhasamuppatti, adukkhama-
sukhā ca yā.
Yato ca bhikkhu ātāpī, sampajaññaṃ na
riñcati
Tato so vedanā sabbā, parijānāti paṇḍito.
So vedanā pariññāya, diṭṭhe dhamme
anāsavo;
Kāyassa bhedā dhammaṭṭho, saṅkhyaṃ
nopeti vedagūti.

Just as various winds blow one by one
through the sky—eastern, western,
northern, and southern, dusty and
dustless, cold and hot, breezes and
gales—many gusts blow,
so too do feelings come about in just
this very body,
arising as pleasant, painful, and neutral.

But a monk who is energetic, intelligent,
and clearly comprehending,
thoroughly understands all feelings.

One thoroughly understanding feelings
is free of destructive predispositions
in this life;
and when the body gives way, one
grounded in truth possesses a
knowledge that cannot be
calculated."

Agārasuttaṃ

Seyyathāpi, bhikkhave, āgantukāgāraṃ. Tattha puratthimāyapi disāya āgantvā vāsaṃ kappenti, pacchimāyapi disāya āgantvā vāsaṃ kappenti, uttarāyapi disāya āgantvā vāsaṃ kappenti, dakkhiṇāyapi disāya āgantvā vāsaṃ kappenti. Khattiyāpi āgantvā vāsaṃ kappenti, brāhmaṇāpi āgantvā vāsaṃ kappenti, vessāpi āgantvā vāsaṃ kappenti, suddāpi āgantvā vāsaṃ kappenti.

Evameva kho, bhikkhave, imasmiṃ kāyasmiṃ vividhā vedanā uppajjanti. Sukhāpi vedanā uppajjati, dukkhāpi vedanā uppajjati, adukkhamasukhāpi vedanā uppajjati. Sāmisāpi sukhā vedanā uppajjati, sāmisāpi dukkhā vedanā uppajjati, sāmisāpi adukkhamasukhā vedanā uppajjati. Nirāmisāpi sukhā vedanā uppajjati, nirāmisāpi dukkhā vedanā uppajjati, nirāmisāpi adukkhamasukhā vedanā uppajjatīti.

The Guest House

"Consider, monks, a guest house. Some people arrive from the east and stay awhile, some arrive from the west and stay awhile, some arrive from the north and stay awhile, and some arrive from the south and stay awhile. Nobles arrive and stay awhile, Brahmin priests arrive and stay awhile, merchants arrive and stay awhile, and servants arrive and stay awhile.[7]

"Similarly, monks, various feelings arise in this body: a pleasant feeling arises, a painful feeling arises, and a neutral feeling arises. A sensory pleasant feeling arises, a sensory painful feeling arises, and a sensory neutral feeling arises. A spiritual pleasant feeling arises, a spiritual painful feeling arises, and a spiritual neutral feeling arises."

▪▪▪

Paṭhamaānandasuttaṃ

Atha kho āyasmā ānando yena bhagavā tenupasaṅkami; upasaṅkamitvā ekamantaṃ nisīdi, ekamantaṃ nisinno kho āyasmā ānando bhagavantaṃ etadavoca—katamā nu kho, bhante, vedanā, katamo vedanāsamudayo, katamo vedanānirodho, katamā vedanānirodhagāminī paṭipadā? Ko vedanāya assādo, ko ādīnavo, kiṃ nissaraṇanti?

Even as they come and go, feelings follow predictable patterns: they arise, they cease, they gratify, they displease; they also have downsides due to the addiction and further pain to which they often lead. They can be eased, quieted, and let go of by giving up the habitual patterns and the craving and desire that propel them.

Ananda

At one time Venerable Ananda approached the Buddha, greeted him cordially, and sat down to one side. Sitting to the side, Ananda spoke to the Buddha: “Sir, what is feeling exactly? What is the arising of feeling? What is the ceasing of feeling? And what is the way leading to the ceasing of feeling? What are the gratification and the downside in feeling? And what is the escape from it?”

Tisso imā, ānanda, vedanā—sukhā vedanā, dukkhā vedanā, adukkhamasukhā vedanā—imā vuccanti, ānanda, vedanā. Phassasamudayā vedanāsamudayo; phassanirodhā vedanānirodho. Ayameva ariyo aṭṭhaṅgiko maggo vedanānirodhagāminī paṭipadā, seyyathidaṃ—sammādiṭṭhi sammāsaṅkappo sammāvācā sammākammanto sammā ājīvo sammāvāyāmo sammāsati sammāsamādhi. Yaṃ vedanaṃ paṭicca uppajjati sukhaṃ somanassaṃ, ayaṃ vedanāya assādo. Yā vedanā aniccā dukkhā vipariṇāmadhammā, ayaṃ vedanāya ādīnavo. Yo vedanāya chandarāgavinayo chandarāgappahānaṃ, idaṃ vedanāya nissaraṇaṃ.

Atha kho panānanda, mayā anupubbasaṅkhārānaṃ nirodho akkhāto . . . pe . . . Atha

"Ananda, there are three kinds of feelings—pleasant feeling, painful feeling, and neutral feeling. These are called feelings, Ananda. With the arising of sensory contact, there is the arising of feeling. With the ceasing of sensory contact, there is the ceasing of feeling. The Noble Eightfold Path—right view, right intention, right speech, right action, right livelihood, right effort, right mindfulness, and right concentration—is the way leading to the ceasing of feeling. The gratification in feeling is pleasure and happiness depending on feeling. The downside of feeling is that feelings are impermanent, suffering, and unstable phenomena. The escape from feeling is the removal of wanting and desire, and the letting go of wanting and desire.

"But, Ananda, I have also described the gradual ceasing of the habitual patterns . . .

kho panānanda, mayā anupubbasaṅkhārānaṃ vūpasamo akkhāto . . . pe . . . Atha kho panānanda, mayā anupubbasaṅkhārānaṃ paṭippassaddhi akkhātā . . . Khīṇāsavassa bhikkhuno rāgo paṭippassaddho hoti, doso paṭippassaddho hoti, moho paṭippassaddho hotīti.

And, Ananda, I have described the gradual calming of the habitual patterns . . . And, Ananda, I have described the gradual quieting of the habitual patterns . . . For the awakened monk, desire is quieted, hatred is quieted, and delusion is quieted."[8]

▪▪▪

The next teaching provides one of the most illuminating discussions of the Buddha's pedagogical methods in the entire Pali Canon. It also suggests something vital about how to approach feeling and emotion. While we might intuitively think that there is a finite number of universal emotions that humans are biologically wired to have, and that each emotion is a basic experience with a distinctive essence or telltale facial expression, contemporary neuroscience is increasingly suggesting that neither idea is correct.

Feelings and emotions are not essences; rather, they are constructed categories. And they are categories that can be described and analyzed variously, depending on the different modes and aspects that are noticed, and, of course, on the purposes of the analysis itself.

The Buddha thought so too. In this teaching he refuses to settle on any single reduction of experience or list of basic feelings. Rather, he is pragmatic in his teaching, giving lists and descriptions of experience only in so far as they are helpful to the context at hand. So we wind up with different lists of feelings, from two types up to one hundred and eight that highlight different aspects for different purposes.[9] *And we need not argue about such lists.*

The discussion concerns whether there are two kinds of feeling (pleasant and painful), or three, adding neutral feelings—literally, those which are neither pleasant nor painful. The issue concerns certain spiritual states that are peacefully beyond pleasant and painful feeling altogether, free of the push-and-pull of feeling. Should these be seen as a type of pleasant feeling since they are peaceful, or are they neutral? The Buddha lets both options stand.

The second half of this teaching picks up the theme that we can reach higher and higher modes of pleasure (sukha) and happiness (somanassa) once we stop tethering our experience to objects of sensory desire. As the mind goes deeper into meditative absorptions it experiences other spheres or dimensions increasingly infinite in nature, beyond consciousness, space, feeling, and perception.[10] *As one advances sequentially through these dimensions, one experiences finer and more sublime pleasures, each finer and more sublime than the last. We begin to see that the further one is removed from sensual pleasure, the more rapturous the bliss becomes.*

It may be difficult for those of us who haven't experienced these rarified meditative states to know quite what to make of them. The beginning student may wish simply to read their descriptions for what they evoke, open to the possibility that the mind is capable of inhabiting extraordinary dimensions not imagined in our ordinary work-a-day lives. As we learn to think with the ancients, we are invited to see that Buddhists found these to be enormously pleasurable precisely because they have nothing to do with sensual pleasure and desire.

To his ascetic rivals who may doubt that these experiences are possible or that they should be conceived as pleasures, the Buddha simply and sublimely insists that "pleasure found anywhere and in whatever way be included in pleasure." He refuses to let go of the category of pleasure even—or perhaps especially—when describing states remote from ordinary conceptions of sensory pleasure.

Pañcakaṅgasuttaṃ

Atha kho pañcakaṅgo thapati yenāyasmā udāyī tenupasaṅkami; upasaṅkamitvā āyasmantaṃ udāyiṃ abhivādetvā ekamantaṃ nisīdi. Ekamantaṃ nisinno kho pañcakaṅgo thapati āyasmantaṃ udāyiṃ etadavoca—kati nu kho, bhante udāyi, vedanā vuttā bhagavatāti?

Tisso kho, thapati, vedanā vuttā bhagavatā. Sukhā vedanā, dukkhā vedanā, adukkhamasukhā vedanā—imā kho, thapati, tisso vedanā vuttā bhagavatāti.

Evaṃ vutte, pañcakaṅgo thapati āyasmantaṃ udāyiṃ etadavoca—na kho, bhante udāyi, tisso vedanā vuttā bhagavatā. Dve vedanā vuttā bhagavatā—sukhā vedanā, dukkhā vedanā. Yāyaṃ, bhante, adukkhamasukhā vedanā, santasmiṃ esā paṇīte sukhe vuttā bhagavatāti.

Panchakanga

Then the master carpenter Panchakanga approached Venerable Udayi, greeted him cordially, and sat down to one side. Sitting to the side, Panchakanga spoke to the Udayi: "Udayi, sir, how many kinds of feelings did the Buddha mention?"

"The Buddha spoke of three kinds of feelings, carpenter. The three kinds of feelings mentioned by the Buddha are pleasant feeling, painful feeling, and neutral feeling."

When told this, the carpenter Panchakanga replied to Udayi: "But sir, the Buddha did not in fact speak of three kinds of feelings. He spoke of two—pleasant feeling and painful feeling. As for the neutral feeling, the Buddha spoke of it in terms of peaceful and sublime pleasure."

Dutiyampi kho āyasmā udāyī pañcakaṅgaṃ thapatiṃ etadavoca—na kho, thapati, dve vedanā vuttā bhagavatā. Tisso vedanā vuttā bhagavatā. Sukhā vedanā, dukkhā vedanā, adukkhamasukhā vedanā—imā tisso vedanā vuttā bhagavatāti. Dutiyampi kho pañcakaṅgo thapati āyasmantaṃ udāyiṃ etadavoca—na kho, bhante udāyi, tisso vedanā vuttā bhagavatā. Dve vedanā vuttā bhagavatā—sukhā vedanā, dukkhā vedanā. Yāyaṃ, bhante, adukkhamasukhā vedanā, santasmiṃ esā paṇīte sukhe vuttā bhagavatāti. Tatiyampi kho . . . Neva sakkhi āyasmā udāyī pañcakaṅgaṃ thapatiṃ saññāpetuṃ, na panāsakkhi pañcakaṅgo thapati āyasmantaṃ udāyiṃ saññāpetuṃ.

Assosi kho āyasmā ānando āyasmato udāyissa pañcakaṅgena thapatinā saddhiṃ imaṃ kathāsallāpaṃ. Atha kho āyasmā ānando yena bhagavā tenupasaṅkami; upasaṅkamitvā eka-

A second time, and then a third time, Venerable Udayi stated his position that the Buddha spoke of three feelings, and the master carpenter Panchakanga stated his position that the Buddha spoke of two feelings, pleasant and painful, and that the neutral feeling was mentioned by the Buddha in terms of peaceful and sublime pleasure.[11] Venerable Udayi was not able to convince the carpenter Panchakanga, and Panchakanga was not able to convince Udayi.

Venerable Ananda came to hear of this conversation between Udayi and Panchakanga. And so Ananda approached the Buddha, greeted him cordially, and sat down to one side. Sitting to the side, Ananda told the Buddha everything about the conversation between Venerable Udayi and the carpenter Panchakanga.

mantaṃ nisīdi. Ekamantaṃ nisinno kho āyasmā ānando yāvatako āyasmato udāyissa pañcakaṅgena thapatinā saddhiṃ ahosi kathāsallāpo taṃ sabbaṃ bhagavato ārocesi.

Santameva, ānanda, pariyāyaṃ pañcakaṅgo thapati udāyissa bhikkhuno nābbhanumodi; santañca panānanda, pariyāyaṃ udāyī bhikkhu pañcakaṅgassa thapatino nābbhanumodi. Dvepi mayā, ānanda, vedanā vuttā pariyāyena. Tissopi mayā vedanā vuttā pariyāyena. Pañcapi mayā vedanā vuttā pariyāyena. Chapi mayā vedanā vuttā pariyāyena. Aṭṭhārasāpi mayā vedanā vuttā pariyāyena. Chattiṃsāpi mayā vedanā vuttā pariyāyena. Aṭṭhasatampi mayā vedanā vuttā pariyāyena.

"Ananda, even though the monk Udayi did not agree, the carpenter Panchakanga's way of putting it is correct. But it is also the case that even though Panchakanga did not agree, the monk Udayi's way of putting it is correct. For I have spoken of two kinds of feelings as one way of putting it, and I have spoken of three kinds of feelings as another way of putting it. Indeed, with different ways of putting it, I have spoken of five kinds of feelings, and I have spoken of six kinds of feelings. I have spoken of eighteen kinds of feelings and I have spoken of thirty-six kinds of feelings. I have also spoken of one hundred and eight kinds of feelings.

Evaṃ pariyāyadesito kho, ānanda, mayā dhammo. Evaṃ pariyāyadesite kho, ānanda, mayā dhamme ye aññamaññassa subhāsitaṃ sulapitaṃ, na samanumaññissanti, na samanujānissanti, na samanumodissanti, tesaṃ etaṃ pāṭikaṅkhaṃ—bhaṇḍanajātā kalahajātā vivādāpannā aññamaññaṃ mukhasattīhi vitudantā viharissanti. Evaṃ pariyāyadesito kho, ānanda, mayā dhammo. Evaṃ pariyāyadesite kho, ānanda, mayā dhamme ye aññamaññassa subhāsitaṃ sulapitaṃ samanumaññissanti samanujānissanti samanumodissanti, tesaṃ etaṃ pāṭikaṅkhaṃ—samaggā sammodamānā avivadamānā khīrodakībhūtā aññamaññaṃ piyacakkhūhi sampassantā viharissantīti.

Pañcime, ānanda, kāmaguṇā. Katame pañca? Cakkhuviññeyyā rūpā iṭṭhā kantā

"Ananda, when I teach the doctrine, I put it differently on different occasions. When I teach the doctrine in different ways it is expected that some people will not agree, concede, and approve what is well spoken and well said by others, and they will become quarrelsome and contentious and fall into arguments. They will spend their time attacking one another with verbal daggers. In this way, Ananda, when I teach the doctrine, I put it in different ways. When I teach the doctrine in different ways, it is expected that other people will agree, concede, and approve what is well spoken and well said by others, and they will live harmoniously, on friendly terms, without contention, and blended like milk and water. They will spend their time seeing one another with benevolent eyes.

"Ananda, there are five objects of sensual pleasure. What are the five? Visual objects manāpā piyarūpā kāmūpasaṃhitā rajanīyā . . . pe . . . sotaviññeyyā saddā . . . pe . . . ghānaviññeyyā gandhā . . . pe . . . jivhāviññeyyā rasā . . . pe . . . kāyaviññeyyā phoṭṭhabbā iṭṭhā kantā manāpā piyarūpā kāmūpasaṃhitā rajanīyā. Ime kho, ānanda, pañca kāmaguṇā.

Yaṃ kho, ānanda, ime pañca kāmaguṇe paṭicca uppajjati sukhaṃ somanassaṃ—idaṃ vuccati kāmasukhaṃ. Ye kho, ānanda, evaṃ vadeyyuṃ—'etaṃparamaṃ santaṃ sukhaṃ somanassaṃ paṭisaṃvedentī'ti—idaṃ nesāhaṃ nānujānāmi. Taṃ kissa hetu? Atthānanda, etamhā sukhā aññaṃ sukhaṃ abhikkantatarañca paṇītatarañca.

perceived by the eye that are desired, enjoyable, charming, agreeable, accompanied with sensual desire, and leading to passion. So too with sounds perceived by the ear, odors perceived by the nose, tastes perceived by the tongue, and tangibles perceived by the body that are desired, enjoyable, charming, agreeable, accompanied by sensual desire, and leading to passion. These, Ananda, are the five objects of sensual pleasure.

"Ananda, when pleasure and happiness occur depending on the five objects of sensual pleasure, this is called sensual pleasure. Some people would say that "This is the highest existing pleasure and happiness that people experience." But I do not agree with them. Why is this? Because there is another pleasure that is finer and more sublime than these pleasures, Ananda.

Katamañcānanda, etamhā sukhā aññaṃ sukhaṃ abhikkantatarañca paṇītatarañca? Idhānanda, bhikkhu vivicceva kāmehi vivicca akusalehi dhammehi savitakkaṃ savicāraṃ vivekajaṃ pītisukhaṃ paṭhamaṃ jhānaṃ upasampajja viharati. Idaṃ kho, ānanda, etamhā sukhā aññaṃ sukhaṃ abhikkantatarañca paṇītatarañca. Ye kho, ānanda, evaṃ vadeyyuṃ—'etaṃparamaṃ santaṃ sukhaṃ somanassaṃ paṭisaṃvedentīti—idaṃ nesāhaṃ nānujānāmi. Taṃ kissa hetu? Atthānanda, etamhā sukhā aññaṃ sukhaṃ abhikkantatarañca paṇītatarañca.

Katamañcānanda, etamhā sukhā aññaṃ sukhaṃ abhikkantatarañca paṇītatarañca? Idhānanda, bhikkhu, vitakkavicārānaṃ vūpasamā ajjhattaṃ sampasādanaṃ cetaso ekodibhāvaṃ avitakkaṃ avicāraṃ samādhijaṃ

"And what, Ananda, is another pleasure that is finer and more sublime than these pleasures? In this case, Ananda, a monk who disengages from sensual pleasures and unhealthy states enters and stays in the first meditative absorption; this includes thought and deliberation and the joy and pleasure that arise from disengaging. This is the pleasure that is finer and more sublime than these pleasures. And so, when some would say that 'This is the highest existing pleasure and happiness that people experience,' I do not agree with them. Why is this? Because there is another pleasure that is finer and more sublime than these pleasures, Ananda.

"And what, Ananda, is another pleasure that is finer and more sublime than these pleasures? In this case, Ananda, a monk enters and stays in the second meditative absorption; this is the joy and pleasure born of

pītisukhaṃ dutiyaṃ jhānaṃ upasampajja viharati. Idaṃ kho, ānanda, etamhā sukhā aññaṃ sukhaṃ abhikkantatarañca paṇītatarañca. Ye kho, ānanda, evaṃ vadeyyuṃ—etaṃparamaṃ santaṃ sukhaṃ somanassaṃ paṭisaṃvedentīti—idaṃ nesāhaṃ nānujānāmi. Taṃ kissa hetu? Atthānanda, etamhā sukhā aññaṃ sukhaṃ abhikkantatarañca paṇītatarañca.

Katamañcānanda, etamhā sukhā aññaṃ sukhaṃ abhikkantatarañca paṇītatarañca? Idhānanda, bhikkhu pītiyā ca virāgā upekkhako ca viharati sato ca sampajāno, sukhañca kāyena paṭisaṃvedeti, yaṃ taṃ ariyā ācikkhanti—upekkhako satimā sukhavihārī'ti tatiyaṃ jhānaṃ upasampajja viharati. Idaṃ kho, ānanda, etamhā sukhā aññaṃ sukhaṃ abhikkantatarañca paṇītatarañca. Ye kho, ānanda,

concentration free of thought and deliberation and is the unification of the mind and the inner clarity that result from the calming of thought and deliberation. This is the pleasure that is finer and more sublime than these pleasures. And so, when some would say that 'This is the highest existing pleasure and happiness that people experience,' I do not agree with them. Why is this? Because there is another pleasure that is finer and more sublime than these pleasures, Ananda.

"And what, Ananda, is another pleasure that is finer and more sublime than these pleasures? In this case, Ananda, a monk enters and stays in the third meditative absorption; this involves the fading away of joy and staying equanimous, mindful, and clearly comprehending while experiencing pleasure with the body. It is described by the noble ones as 'equanimous, mindful, and

evaṃ vadeyyuṃ—'etaṃparamaṃ santaṃ sukhaṃ somanassaṃ paṭisaṃvedentīti—idaṃ nesāhaṃ nānujānāmi. Taṃ kissa hetu? Atthānanda, etamhā sukhā aññaṃ sukhaṃ abhikkantatarañca paṇītatarañca.

Katamañcānanda, etamhā sukhā aññaṃ sukhaṃ abhikkantatarañca paṇītatarañca? Idhānanda, bhikkhu sukhassa ca pahānā dukkhassa ca pahānā pubbeva somanassadomanassānaṃ atthaṅgamā adukkhamasukhaṃ upekkhāsatipārisuddhiṃ catutthaṃ jhānaṃ upasampajja viharati. Idaṃ kho, ānanda, etamhā sukhā aññaṃ sukhaṃ abhikkantatarañca paṇītatarañca. Ye kho, ānanda, evaṃ vadeyyuṃ—etaṃparamaṃ santaṃ sukhaṃ somanassaṃ paṭisaṃvedentīti—idaṃ nesāhaṃ nānujānāmi. Taṃ kissa hetu? At-

spending time pleasurably.' This is the pleasure that is finer and more sublime than these pleasures. And so, when some would say that 'This is the highest existing pleasure and happiness that people experience,' I do not agree with them. Why is this? Because there is another pleasure that is finer and more sublime than these pleasures, Ananda.

"And what, Ananda, is another pleasure that is finer and more sublime than these pleasures? In this case, Ananda, a monk enters and stays in the fourth meditative absorption; this is the purification of mindfulness by equanimity and is neither pleasant nor painful due to the subsiding of happiness and distress from previously letting go of pleasure and pain. This is the pleasure that is finer and more sublime than these pleasures. And so, when some would say that 'This is the highest existing pleasure

thānanda, etamhā sukhā aññaṃ sukhaṃ abhikkantatarañca paṇītatarañca.

Katamañcānanda, etamhā sukhā aññaṃ sukhaṃ abhikkantatarañca paṇītatarañca? Idhānanda, bhikkhu sabbaso rūpasaññānaṃ samatikkamā, paṭighasaññānaṃ atthaṅgamā, nānattasaññānaṃ amanasikārā, ananto ākāsoti ākāsānañcāyatanaṃ upasampajja viharati. Idaṃ kho, ānanda, etamhā sukhā aññaṃ sukhaṃ abhikkantatarañca paṇītatarañca. Ye kho, ānanda, evaṃ vadeyyuṃ—etaṃparamaṃ santaṃ sukhaṃ somanassaṃ paṭisaṃvedentīti—idaṃ nesāhaṃ nānujānāmi. Taṃ kissa hetu? Atthānanda, etamhā sukhā aññaṃ sukhaṃ abhikkantatarañca paṇītatarañca.

and happiness that people experience,' I do not agree with them. Why is this? Because there is another pleasure that is finer and more sublime than these pleasures, Ananda.

"And what, Ananda, is another pleasure that is finer and more sublime than these pleasures? In this case, Ananda, a monk, by going entirely beyond the perception of visual forms, by the settling down of the perception of sensory impact, and by the lack of attention paid to the perception of multiplicity, is aware that 'space is infinite,' and so enters and stays in the dimension of infinite space. This is the pleasure that is finer and more sublime than these pleasures. And so, when some would say that 'This is the highest existing pleasure and happiness that people experience,' I do not agree with them. Why is this? Because there is another pleasure that is finer and more sublime than these pleasures, Ananda.

Katamañcānanda, etamhā sukhā aññaṃ sukhaṃ abhikkantatarañca paṇītatarañca? Idhānanda, bhikkhu sabbaso ākāsānañcāyatanaṃ samatikkamma, anantaṃ viññāṇanti viññāṇañcāyatanaṃ upasampajja viharati. Idaṃ kho, ānanda, etamhā sukhā aññaṃ sukhaṃ abhikkantatarañca paṇītatarañca. Ye kho, ānanda, evaṃ vadeyyuṃ—etaṃparamaṃ santaṃ sukhaṃ somanassaṃ paṭisaṃvedentīti—idaṃ nesāhaṃ nānujānāmi. Taṃ kissa hetu? Atthānanda, etamhā sukhā aññaṃ sukhaṃ abhikkantatarañca paṇītatarañca.

Katamañcānanda, etamhā sukhā aññaṃ sukhaṃ abhikkantatarañca paṇītatarañca? Idhānanda, bhikkhu sabbaso viññāṇañcāyatanaṃ samatikkamma, natthi kiñcīti ākiñcaññāyatanaṃ upasampajja viharati.

"And what, Ananda, is another pleasure that is finer and more sublime than these pleasures? In this case, Ananda, a monk, by going entirely beyond the dimension of infinite space, is aware that 'consciousness is infinite,' and so enters and stays in the dimension of infinite consciousness. This is the pleasure that is finer and more sublime than these pleasures. And so, when some would say that 'This is the highest existing pleasure and happiness that people experience,' I do not agree with them. Why is this? Because there is another pleasure that is finer and more sublime than these pleasures, Ananda.

"And what, Ananda, is another pleasure that is finer and more sublime than these pleasures? In this case, Ananda, a monk, by going entirely beyond the dimension of infinite consciousness, is aware that 'there is

Idaṃ kho, ānanda, etamhā sukhā aññaṃ sukhaṃ abhikkantatarañca paṇītatarañca. Ye kho, ānanda, evaṃ vadeyyuṃ—'etaṃparamaṃ santaṃ sukhaṃ somanassaṃ paṭisaṃvedentī'ti—idaṃ nesāhaṃ nānujānāmi. Taṃ kissa hetu? Atthānanda, etamhā sukhā aññaṃ sukhaṃ abhikkantatarañca paṇītatarañca.

Katamañcānanda, etamhā sukhā aññaṃ sukhaṃ abhikkantatarañca paṇītatarañca? Idhānanda, bhikkhu sabbaso ākiñcaññāyatanaṃ samatikkamma nevasaññānāsaññāyatanaṃ upasampajja viharati. Idaṃ kho, ānanda, etamhā sukhā aññaṃ sukhaṃ abhikkantatarañca paṇītatarañca. Ye kho, ānanda, evaṃ vadeyyuṃ—etaṃparamaṃ santaṃ sukhaṃ somanassaṃ paṭisaṃvedentīti—idaṃ nesāhaṃ nānujānāmi. Taṃ kissa hetu? Atthānanda, etamhā

nothing,' and so enters and stays in the dimension of nothingness. This the pleasure that is finer and more sublime than these pleasures. And so, when some would say that 'This is the highest existing pleasure and happiness that people experience,' I do not agree with them. Why is this? Because there is another pleasure that is finer and more sublime than these pleasures, Ananda.

"And what, Ananda, is another pleasure that is finer and more sublime than these pleasures? In this case, Ananda, a monk, by going entirely beyond the dimension of nothingness, enters and stays in the dimension of neither perception nor nonperception. This is the pleasure that is finer and more sublime than these pleasures. And so, when some would say that 'This is the highest existing pleasure and happiness that people experience,' I do not agree with

sukhā aññaṃ sukhaṃ abhikkantatarañca paṇītatarañca.

Katamañcānanda, etamhā sukhā aññaṃ sukhaṃ abhikkantatarañca paṇītatarañca? Idhānanda, bhikkhu sabbaso nevasaññānāsaññāyatanaṃ samatikkamma saññāvedayitanirodhaṃ upasampajja viharati. Idaṃ kho, ānanda, etamhā sukhā aññaṃ sukhaṃ abhikkantatarañca paṇītatarañca.

Ṭhānaṃ kho panetaṃ, ānanda, vijjati yaṃ aññatitthiyā paribbājakā evaṃ vadeyyuṃ—saññāvedayitanirodhaṃ samaṇo gotamo āha, tañca sukhasmiṃ paññapeti. Tayidaṃ kiṃsu, tayidaṃ kathaṃsūti?

Evaṃvādino, ānanda, aññatitthiyā paribbājakā evamassu vacanīyā—na kho, āvuso,

them. Why is this? Because there is another pleasure that is finer and more sublime than these pleasures, Ananda.

"And what, Ananda, is another pleasure that is finer and more sublime than these pleasures? In this case, Ananda, a monk, by going entirely beyond the dimension of neither perception nor nonperception, enters and stays in the ceasing of perception and feeling. This, Ananda, is the pleasure that is finer and more sublime than these pleasures.

"But it is possible, Ananda, that renunciants belonging to other sects might say 'The recluse Gotama speaks of the ceasing of perception and feeling and teaches that it is included in pleasure. What is this and how can it be?'

"Those renunciants belonging to other sects who say this should be told: 'Friends,

bhagavā sukhaññeva vedanaṃ sandhāya sukhasmiṃ paññapeti. Yattha yattha, āvuso, sukhaṃ upalabbhati, yahiṃ yahiṃ taṃ taṃ tathāgato sukhasmiṃ paññapetīti.

the Buddha does not teach of states included in pleasure only with reference to pleasant feeling. Rather, the Buddha teaches that pleasure found anywhere and in whatever way is included in pleasure.'"

▪▪▪

The following passage considers the causes of feelings from a different perspective than the psychological model of dependent arising. It introduces karma (action or the result of action). The idea of karma points to the causal nature of our experience, whereby much of what we experience arises from moral conditions in the past and, in turn, generates the conditions for further experience. But in this important passage, the Buddha refuses to say that all experience is the result of karma. That would be overreaching what is actually known and said to be true.

Sīvakasuttaṃ

Ekaṃ samayaṃ bhagavā rājagahe viharati veḷuvane kalandakanivāpe. Atha kho moḷiyasīvako paribbājako yena bhagavā tenupasaṅkami; upasaṅkamitvā bhagavatā saddhiṃ sammodi. Sammodanīyaṃ kathaṃ sāraṇīyaṃ vītisāretvā ekamantaṃ nisīdi. Ekamantaṃ nisinno kho moḷiyasīvako paribbājako bhagavantaṃ etadavoca—santi, bho gotama, eke samaṇabrāhmaṇā evaṃvādino evaṃdiṭṭhino—yaṃ kiñcāyaṃ purisapuggalo paṭisaṃvedeti sukhaṃ vā dukkhaṃ vā adukkhamasukhaṃ vā sabbaṃ taṃ pubbekatahetūti. Idha bhavaṃ gotamo kimāhāti?

Many feelings come about from the "humors"—bile, phlegm, and wind—or a combination of them (according to Ayurvedic theories of health), or from other causes that have nothing to do with karma.

Sivaka

Once the Buddha was staying in the Bamboo Forest at Squirrel Park in Rajagaha. Then, Sivaka of the Top-knot, the wanderer, approached the Buddha and exchanged greetings. The talk was cordial, and when they had finished their pleasantries, he sat to one side. Sitting to the side, Sivaka of the Top-Knot said to the Buddha: "Gotama, there are some ascetics and Brahmins[12] holding this doctrine and view, namely that 'Anything an individual person feels—whether pleasant, painful, or neutral—is completely caused by past action.' What does Gotama say about this?"

Pittasamuṭṭhānānipi kho, sīvaka, idhekaccāni vedayitāni uppajjanti. Sāmampi kho etaṃ, sīvaka, veditabbaṃ yathā pittasamuṭṭhānānipi idhekaccāni vedayitāni uppajjanti; lokassapi kho etaṃ, sīvaka, saccasammataṃ yathā pittasamuṭṭhānānipi idhekaccāni vedayitāni uppajjanti. Tatra, sīvaka, ye te samaṇabrāhmaṇā evaṃvādino evaṃdiṭṭhino—yaṃ kiñcāyaṃ purisapuggalo paṭisaṃvedeti sukhaṃ vā dukkhaṃ vā adukkhamasukhaṃ vā sabbaṃ taṃ pubbekatahetūti. Yañca sāmaṃ ñātaṃ tañca atidhāvanti, yañca loke saccasammataṃ tañca atidhāvanti. Tasmā tesaṃ samaṇabrāhmaṇānaṃ micchāti vadāmi.

Semhasamuṭṭhānānipi kho, sīvaka . . . pe . . . vātasamuṭṭhānānipi kho, sīvaka . . . pe . . . sannipātikānipi kho, sīvaka . . . pe . . . utupariṇāmajānipi kho, sīvaka . . . pe . . . visamaparihārajānipi kho, sīvaka . . . pe . . . opakkamikānipi kho, sīvaka . . . pe . . . kammavi-

"Sivaka, some feelings that occur originate in bile. One can know for oneself, Sivaka, that some feelings that occur originate in bile, and ordinary people accept that some feelings originate in bile. In this case, Sivaka, when ascetics and Brahmins hold the doctrine and view that anything an individual person feels—whether pleasant, painful, or neutral—is completely caused by past action, they overstate what they actually know, and they go beyond what ordinary people accept. Therefore, I say that those ascetics and Brahmins are wrong.

"Sivaka, there are also feelings that originate in phlegm, wind, or a combination of the three humors. And some are due to a change in the seasons, carelessness, or assault. And some are produced as a result of karma. This can be known for oneself, Sivaka. And that some feelings are produced

pākajānipi kho, sīvaka, idhekaccāni vedayitāni uppajjanti. Sāmampi kho etaṃ, sīvaka, veditabbaṃ. Yathā kammavipākajānipi idhekaccāni vedayitāni uppajjanti; lokassapi kho etaṃ, sīvaka, saccasammataṃ. Yathā kammavipākajānipi idhekaccāni vedayitāni uppajjanti; tatra, sīvaka, ye te samaṇabrāhmaṇā evaṃvādino evaṃdiṭṭhino—yaṃ kiñcāyaṃ purisapuggalo paṭisaṃvedeti sukhaṃ vā dukkhaṃ vā adukkhamasukhaṃ vā sabbaṃ taṃ pubbekatahetūti. Yañca sāmaṃ ñātaṃ tañca atidhāvanti yañca loke saccasammataṃ tañca atidhāvanti. Tasmā tesaṃ samaṇabrāhmaṇānaṃ micchāti vadāmīti. Evaṃ vutte, moḷiyasīvako paribbājako bhagavantaṃ etadavoca—abhikkantaṃ, bho gotama, abhikkantaṃ, bho gotama . . . pe . . . upāsakaṃ maṃ bhavaṃ gotamo dhāretu ajjatagge pāṇupetaṃ saraṇaṃ gatanti.

as a result of karma is known to be true by the world. And so, when ascetics and Brahmins hold the doctrine and view that anything an individual person feels—whether pleasant, painful, or neutral—is completely caused by past action, they overstate what they actually know, and they go beyond what ordinary people accept. Therefore, I say that those ascetics and Brahmins are wrong."

When this was said, Sivaka of the Topknot, the wanderer, told the Buddha: "Excellent, Gotama, excellent! May Gotama consider me a lay follower, taking refuge from this day forward until I die."

Pittaṃ semhañca vāto ca, sannipātā utūni ca;
Visamaṃ opakkamikaṃ, kammavipākena aṭṭhamīti.

These are eight causes of feeling:
bile, phlegm, wind, and their combination; the seasons, uneven care, assault, and the results of karma.

■ ■ ■

In the discussion above between Panchakanga and Udayi, the Buddha says that there are many ways of putting the doctrine whereby we can arrive at various lists of feelings—two, three, five, six, eighteen, thirty-six, and one hundred and eight. There are different ways of slicing and dicing feelings for observation and analysis. And there are different modalities in which they occur. The next passage follows up on this, stipulating the different taxonomies and descriptions that yield different ways of attending to feelings.

This may involve distinguishing between feelings as bodily or mental, or by where and how they occur in terms of each of the six senses.

And we can go beyond analyzing feelings as valences and see them as including "emotions," such as happiness and distress, while noting that Pali has no exact or even close correlate of the category of emotions. Feelings can also be "faculties," or capabilities with which we construct experience. We are not just passive recipients of feelings assailing us. Rather, a feeling can also be an aptitude or prediction whereby we construct and create what we feel, based on our proclivities for pleasure, pain, happiness, distress, or equanimity. We know that people have different responses to the same stimuli, depending on what they bring to it. The same piece of music will be pleasurable for some and disagreeable to others based on their background, capacity, and preconditions. Some find a certain cuisine tasty and delicious, while others are completely put off by it. Feelings can thus include ways we "approach" the world. We come to sensory experience predisposed to happiness, distress, or equanimity, conditions that help create what we feel.

Feelings and emotions are also usefully classified according to whether they are based on the household life (where sensual pleasures dominate) or the monastic life (which ideally involves meditative pleasures). And we can watch feelings across time, noting past, present, and possible future feelings.

Aṭṭhasatasuttaṃ

Aṭṭhasatapariyāyaṃ vo, bhikkhave, dhammapariyāyaṃ desessāmi. Taṃ suṇātha. Katamo ca, bhikkhave, aṭṭhasatapariyāyo, dhammapariyāyo? Dvepi mayā, bhikkhave, vedanā vuttā pariyāyena; tissopi mayā vedanā vuttā pariyāyena; pañcapi mayā vedanā vuttā pariyāyena; chapi mayā vedanā vuttā pariyāyena; aṭṭhārasāpi mayā vedanā vuttā pariyāyena; chattiṃsāpi mayā vedanā vuttā pariyāyena; aṭṭhasatampi mayā vedanā vuttā pariyāyena.

"Katamā ca, bhikkhave, dve vedanā? Kāyikā ca cetasikā ca—imā vuccanti, bhikkhave, dve vedanā. Katamā ca, bhikkhave, tisso ve-

One Hundred and Eight

"Monks, I will teach you a way of putting the doctrine in terms of one hundred and eight kinds of feelings. Please listen to this. And what, monks, is a way of putting the doctrine in terms of one hundred and eight? I have spoken in terms of two kinds of feelings; and I have spoken in terms of three kinds of feelings; and I have spoken in terms of five kinds of feelings; and I have spoken in terms of six kinds of feelings; and I have spoken also in terms of eighteen kinds of feelings; and I have spoken also in terms of thirty-six kinds of feelings. And I have also spoken in terms of one hundred and eight kinds of feelings.

"What are the two kinds of feelings, monks? Bodily and mental—these are said to be the two kinds of feelings.

danā? Sukhā vedanā, dukkhā vedanā, adukkhamasukhā vedanā—imā vuccanti, bhikkhave, tisso vedanā. Katamā ca, bhikkhave, pañca vedanā? Sukhindriyaṃ, dukkhindriyaṃ, somanassindriyaṃ, domanassindriyaṃ, upekkhindriyaṃ—imā vuccanti, bhikkhave, pañca vedanā. Katamā ca, bhikkhave, cha vedanā? Cakkhusamphassajā vedanā . . . pe . . . manosamphassajā vedanā—imā vuccanti, bhikkhave, cha vedanā. Katamā ca, bhikkhave, aṭṭhārasa vedanā? Cha somanassūpavicārā, cha domanassūpavicārā, cha upekkhūpavicārā—imā vuccanti, bhikkhave, aṭṭhārasa vedanā. Katamā ca, bhikkhave, chattiṃsa vedanā? Cha gehasitāni somanassāni, cha nekkhammasitāni somanassāni, cha gehasitāni domanassāni, cha nekkhammasitāni domanassāni, cha gehasitā upekkhā, cha nekkhammasitā upekkhā—imā vuccanti, bhikkhave, chattiṃsa vedanā. Katamañca,

"What are the three kinds of feelings, monks? Pleasant feeling, painful feeling, and neutral feeling—these are said to be the three kinds of feelings.

"What are the five kinds of feelings, monks? The faculty of pleasure, the faculty of pain, the faculty of happiness, the faculty of distress, and the faculty of equanimity—these are said to be the five kinds of feelings.

"What are the six kinds of feelings, monks? Feelings born from visual contact, and those born of contact with the other four senses, as well as feelings born from contact with the mind—these are said to be the six kinds of feelings.[13]

"What are the eighteen kinds of feelings, monks? The six ways of approaching things with happiness, the six ways of approaching things with distress, and the six ways of approaching things with equanimity—these

bhikkhave, aṭṭhasataṃ vedanā? Atītā chattiṃsa vedanā, anāgatā chattiṃsa vedanā, paccuppannā chattiṃsa vedanā—imā vuccanti, bhikkhave, aṭṭhasataṃ vedanā. Ayaṃ, bhikkhave, aṭṭhasatapariyāyo dhammapariyāyo"ti.

are said to be the eighteen kinds of feelings.[14]

"What are the thirty-six kinds of feelings, monks? The six happinesses of a household life, the six happinesses of a life of letting things go, the six distresses of a household life, the six distresses of a life of letting things go, the six kinds of equanimity associated with household life, the six kinds of equanimity associated with a life of letting things go—these are said to be the thirty-six kinds of feelings.[15]

"And what, monks, are the one hundred and eight kinds of feelings? The thirty-six feelings of the past, the thirty-six feelings of the future, and the thirty-six feelings of the present—these are said to be the one hundred and eight feelings. This, monks, is a way of putting the doctrine in terms of one hundred and eight."

▪▪▪

The following two passages together suggest two key ideas. First, the Buddha's awakening experience, when he came to see the Four Noble Truths concerning feeling, is presented as a discovery. He came to know feeling, how it arises, and what leads to it. Knowing what leads to it, he learned how it ceases as the conditions generating it cease. He came to see the "way" to quiet feeling, alluding to the Noble Eightfold Path of coming to be free of suffering. And he saw the cycles of gratification and the downside of feeling; ultimately he saw the escape from feeling altogether.

The passage immediately following this one, however, suggests that although the Buddha made these deep discoveries, the knowledge of feelings he teaches is not exclusive to him. Any teacher can track these processes and thus come to know them as they really are.

Ñāṇasuttaṃ

Imā vedanā'ti me, bhikkhave, pubbe ananussutesu dhammesu cakkhuṃ udapādi, ñāṇaṃ udapādi, paññā udapādi, vijjā udapādi, āloko udapādi. 'Ayaṃ vedanāsamudayo'ti me, bhikkhave, pubbe ananussutesu dhammesu cakkhuṃ udapādi . . . pe . . . āloko udapādi. 'Ayaṃ vedanāsamudayagāminī paṭipadā'ti me, bhikkhave, pubbe ananussutesu dhammesu cakkhuṃ udapādi . . . pe . . . 'ayaṃ vedanānirodho'ti me, bhikkhave, pubbe ananussutesu dhammesu cakkhuṃ udapādi . . . pe . . . 'ayaṃ vedanānirodhagāminī paṭipadā'ti me, bhikkhave, pubbe ananussutesu dhammesu cakkhuṃ udapādi . . . pe . . . 'ayaṃ vedanāya assādo'ti me, bhikkhave, pubbe ananussutesu dhammesu . . . pe . . . 'ayaṃ vedanāya ādīnavo'ti me, bhikkhave, pubbe ananussutesu dhammesu . . . pe . . . 'idaṃ kho nissaraṇa'nti me, bhikkhave, pubbe ananus-

Knowledge

"With regard to things not heard before, vision arose, knowledge arose, understanding arose, wisdom arose, and clarity arose as I realized: *These are feelings.* With regard to things not heard before, vision arose, knowledge arose, understanding arose, wisdom arose, and clarity arose as I realized: *This is the origin of feeling.* With regard to things not heard before, vision arose, knowledge arose, understanding arose, wisdom arose, and clarity arose as I realized: *This is the way leading to the origin of feeling.* With regard to things not heard before, vision arose, knowledge arose, understanding arose, wisdom arose, and clarity arose as I realized: *This is the ceasing of feeling.* With regard to things not heard before, vision arose, knowledge arose, understanding arose, wisdom arose, and clarity arose as I

sutesu dhammesu cakkhuṃ udapādi, ñāṇaṃ udapādi, paññā udapādi, vijjā udapādi, āloko udapādī"ti.

Paṭhamasamaṇabrāhmaṇasuttaṃ

Tisso imā, bhikkhave, vedanā. Katamā tisso? Sukhā vedanā, dukkhā vedanā, adukkhamasukhā vedanā. Ye hi keci, bhikkhave, samaṇā vā brāhmaṇā vā imāsaṃ tissannaṃ vedanānaṃ samudayañca atthaṅgamañca assādañca ādīnavañca nissaraṇañca yathābhūtaṃ nappajānanti. Na me te, bhikkhave, samaṇā vā brāhmaṇā vā samaṇesu vā samaṇasammatā brāhmaṇesu vā brāhmaṇasammatā, na ca pana te āyasmanto sāmaññatthaṃ vā brah-

realized: *This is the way leading to the ceasing of feeling.* With regard to things not heard before, vision arose, knowledge arose, understanding arose, wisdom arose, and clarity arose as I realized: *This is the gratification in feelings, this is the downside in feelings, and this is the escape from feelings.*"[16]

Ascetics and Brahmins

"Monks, there are three kinds of feelings. What are the three? Pleasant feeling, painful feeling, and neutral feeling. But there are some ascetics and Brahmins who do not understand as they really are the arising of, the subsiding of, the gratification in, the downside in, and the escape from these three feelings. I do not consider them ascetics among ascetics or Brahmins among Brahmins, and these venerable ones, not having personally and with

maññatthaṃ vā diṭṭheva dhamme sayaṃ abhiññā sacchikatvā upasampajja viharanti.

Ye ca kho keci, bhikkhave, samaṇā vā brāhmaṇā vā imāsaṃ tissannaṃ vedanānaṃ samudayañca atthaṅgamañca assādañca ādīnavaṃ ca nissaraṇañca yathābhūtaṃ pajānanti. Te kho me, bhikkhave, samaṇā vā brāhmaṇā vā samaṇesu ceva samaṇasammatā brāhmaṇesu ca brāhmaṇasammatā. Te ca panāyasmanto sāmaññatthañca brahmaññatthañca, diṭṭheva dhamme sayaṃ abhiññā sacchikatvā upasampajja viharantīti.

their own direct knowledge experienced these evident phenomena, do not enter into and live the goal of asceticism or the goal of being a Brahmin.

"But there are also some ascetics and Brahmins who understand the arising of, the subsiding of, the gratification in, the downside in, and the escape from these three feelings as they really are. I consider them ascetics among ascetics and Brahmins among Brahmins, and these venerable ones, having personally and with their own direct knowledge experienced these evident phenomena, enter into and live the goal of asceticism and the goal of being a Brahmin."

■■■

The final passage in "Teachings on Feelings" returns us to sukha—pleasure, happiness, bliss—and the distinctions between sensory

Nirāmisasuttaṃ

Atthi, bhikkhave, sāmisā pīti, atthi nirāmisā pīti, atthi nirāmisā nirāmisatarā pīti; atthi sāmisaṃ sukhaṃ, atthi nirāmisaṃ sukhaṃ, atthi nirāmisā nirāmisataraṃ sukhaṃ; atthi sāmisā upekkhā, atthi nirāmisā upekkhā, atthi nirāmisā nirāmisatarā upekkhā; atthi sāmiso

forms of sukha and escalating spiritual forms of it. We also find the joy, equanimity, and freedom that can occur in both sensual and spiritual varieties.

Spiritual forms of joy, pleasure, equanimity, and freedom are found in the meditative absorptions and the higher dimensions. But there are also forms of these "more spiritual than the spiritual," as in the ultimate state of nirvana where all desire, hatred, and delusion are vanquished entirely. This is highest freedom.

Spiritual Things

"Monks, there is sensory joy, there is spiritual joy, and there is joy that is more spiritual than the spiritual. There is sensory pleasure, there is spiritual pleasure, and there is pleasure that is more spiritual than the spiritual. There is sensory equanimity,

vimokkho, atthi nirāmiso vimokkho, atthi nirāmisā nirāmisataro vimokkho.

Katamā ca, bhikkhave, sāmisā pīti? Pañcime, bhikkhave, kāmaguṇā. Katame pañca? Cakkhuviññeyyā rūpā iṭṭhā kantā manāpā piyarūpā kāmūpasaṃhitā rajanīyā . . . pe . . . kāyaviññeyyā phoṭṭhabbā iṭṭhā kantā manāpā piyarūpā kāmūpasaṃhitā rajanīyā. Ime kho, bhikkhave, pañca kāmaguṇā. Yā kho, bhikkhave, ime pañca kāmaguṇe paṭicca uppajjati pīti, ayaṃ vuccati, bhikkhave, sāmisā pīti.

Katamā ca, bhikkhave, nirāmisā pīti? Idha, bhikkhave, bhikkhu vivicceva kāmehi vivicca

there is spiritual equanimity, and there is equanimity that is more spiritual than the spiritual. There is sensory freedom, there is spiritual freedom, and there is freedom that is more spiritual than spiritual.

"And what, monks, is sensory joy? There are five objects of sensual pleasure. What are the five? Visual objects perceived by the eye that are desired, enjoyable, charming, agreeable, accompanied by sensual desire, and leading to passion. So too the other sense objects perceived by the other senses and the body that are desired, enjoyable, charming, agreeable, accompanied by sensual desire, and leading to passion. These are the five objects of sensual pleasure. Sensory joy, monks, is called the joy that occurs dependent on these five objects of sensual pleasure.

"And what, monks, is spiritual joy? In this case, a monk disengaging from sensual

akusalehi dhammehi savitakkaṃ savicāraṃ vivekajaṃ pītisukhaṃ paṭhamaṃ jhānaṃ upasampajja viharati. Vitakkavicārānaṃ vūpasamā ajjhattaṃ sampasādanaṃ cetaso ekodibhāvaṃ avitakkaṃ avicāraṃ samādhijaṃ pītisukhaṃ dutiyaṃ jhānaṃ upasampajja viharati. Ayaṃ vuccati, bhikkhave, nirāmisā pīti.

Katamā ca, bhikkhave, nirāmisā nirāmisatarā pīti? Yā kho, bhikkhave, khīṇāsavassa bhikkhuno rāgā cittaṃ vimuttaṃ paccavekkhato, dosā cittaṃ vimuttaṃ paccavekkhato, mohā cittaṃ vimuttaṃ paccavekkhato uppajjati pīti, ayaṃ vuccati, bhikkhave, nirāmisā nirāmisatarā pīti.

pleasures and disengaging from unhealthy states, enters and stays in the first meditative absorption that includes thought and deliberation and the joy and pleasure that arise from disengaging. He enters and stays in the second meditative absorption; this is the joy and pleasure born of concentration free of thought and deliberation and is the unification of the mind and the inner clarity that results from the calming of thought and deliberation. This is called spiritual joy, monks.

"And what, monks, is joy that is more spiritual than spiritual? For an awakened monk contemplating a mind free of desire, contemplating a mind free of hatred, contemplating a mind free of delusion, joy arises. This is called a joy more spiritual than spiritual.

Katamañca, bhikkhave, sāmisaṃ sukhaṃ? Pañcime, bhikkhave, kāmaguṇā. Katame pañca? Cakkhuviññeyyā rūpā iṭṭhā kantā manāpā piyarūpā kāmūpasaṃhitā rajanīyā . . . pe . . . kāyaviññeyyā phoṭṭhabbā iṭṭhā kantā manāpā piyarūpā kāmūpasaṃhitā rajanīyā. Ime kho, bhikkhave, pañca kāmaguṇā. Yaṃ kho, bhikkhave, ime pañca kāmaguṇe paṭicca uppajjati sukhaṃ somanassaṃ, idaṃ vuccati, bhikkhave, sāmisaṃ sukhaṃ.

Katamañca, bhikkhave, nirāmisaṃ sukhaṃ? Idha, bhikkhave, bhikkhu vivicceva kāmehi vivicca akusalehi dhammehi savitakkaṃ savicāraṃ vivekajaṃ pītisukhaṃ paṭhamaṃ jhānaṃ upasampajja viharati. Vi-

"And what, monks, is sensory pleasure? There are five objects of sensual pleasure. What are the five? Visual objects perceived by the eye that are desired, enjoyable, charming, agreeable, accompanied by sensual desire, and leading to passion. So too, the other sense objects perceived by the other senses and the body that are desired, enjoyable, charming, agreeable, accompanied by sensual desire, and leading to passion. These are the five objects of sensual pleasure. Sensory pleasure, monks, is called the pleasure that is happiness occurring dependent on these five objects of sensual pleasure.

"And what, monks, is spiritual pleasure? In this case, a monk disengaging from sensual pleasures and disengaging from unhealthy states, enters and stays in the first meditative absorption that includes thought

takkavicārānaṃ vūpasamā ajjhattaṃ sampasādanaṃ cetaso ekodibhāvaṃ avitakkaṃ avicāraṃ samādhijaṃ pītisukhaṃ dutiyaṃ jhānaṃ upasampajja viharati. Pītiyā ca virāgā upekkhako ca viharati sato ca sampajāno sukhañca kāyena paṭisaṃvedeti, yaṃ taṃ ariyā ācikkhanti—upekkhako satimā sukhavihārīti tatiyaṃ jhānaṃ upasampajja viharati. Idaṃ vuccati, bhikkhave, nirāmisaṃ sukhaṃ.

Katamañca, bhikkhave, nirāmisā nirāmisataraṃ sukhaṃ? Yaṃ kho, bhikkhave, khīṇāsavassa bhikkhuno rāgā cittaṃ vimuttaṃ paccavekkhato, dosā cittaṃ vimuttaṃ pac-

and deliberation and the joy and pleasure that arise from disengaging. He enters and stays in the second meditative absorption that includes the joy and pleasure born of concentration free of thought and deliberation, where the mind is unified and has the inner clarity that results from the calming of thought and deliberation. He enters and stays in the third meditative absorption that involves the fading away of joy and staying equanimous, mindful, and clearly comprehending while experiencing pleasure with the body. It is described by the noble ones as 'equanimous, mindful, and spending time pleasurably.' This is called spiritual pleasure, monks.

"And what, monks, is pleasure that is more spiritual than spiritual? For an awakened monk contemplating a mind free of desire, contemplating a mind free of hatred, con-

cavekkhato, mohā cittaṃ vimuttaṃ paccavekkhato uppajjati sukhaṃ somanassaṃ, idaṃ vuccati, bhikkhave, nirāmisā nirāmisataraṃ sukhaṃ.

Katamā ca, bhikkhave, sāmisā upekkhā? Pañcime, bhikkhave, kāmaguṇā. Katame pañca? Cakkhuviññeyyā rūpā iṭṭhā kantā manāpā piyarūpā kāmūpasaṃhitā rajanīyā . . . pe . . . kāyaviññeyyā phoṭṭhabbā iṭṭhā kantā manāpā piyarūpā kāmūpasaṃhitā rajanīyā. Ime kho, bhikkhave, pañca kāmaguṇā. Yā kho, bhikkhave, ime pañca kāmaguṇe paṭicca uppajjati upekkhā, ayaṃ vuccati, bhikkhave, sāmisā upekkhā.

Katamā ca, bhikkhave, nirāmisā upekkhā? Idha, bhikkhave, bhikkhu sukhassa ca pahānā,

templating a mind free of delusion, a pleasure that is happiness arises. This is called the pleasure more spiritual than spiritual.

"And what, monks, is sensory equanimity? There are five objects of sensual pleasure. What are the five? Visual objects perceived by the eye that are desired, enjoyable, charming, agreeable, accompanied by sensual desire, and leading to passion. So too the other sense objects perceived by the other senses and the body that are desired, enjoyable, charming, agreeable, accompanied by sensual desire, and leading to passion. These are the five objects of sensual pleasure. Sensory equanimity, monks, is called the equanimity occurring dependent on these five objects of sensual pleasure.

"And what, monks, is spiritual equanimity? In this case, Ananda, a monk enters and stays

dukkhassa ca pahānā, pubbeva somanassadomanassānaṃ atthaṅgamā, adukkhamasukhaṃ upekkhāsatipārisuddhiṃ catutthaṃ jhānaṃ upasampajja viharati. Ayaṃ vuccati, bhikkhave, nirāmisā upekkhā.

Katamā ca, bhikkhave, nirāmisā nirāmisatarā upekkhā? Yā kho, bhikkhave, khīṇāsavassa bhikkhuno rāgā cittaṃ vimuttaṃ paccavekkhato, dosā cittaṃ vimuttaṃ paccavekkhato, mohā cittaṃ vimuttaṃ paccavekkhato uppajjati upekkhā, ayaṃ vuccati, bhikkhave, nirāmisā nirāmisatarā upekkhā.

Katamo ca, bhikkhave, sāmiso vimokkho? Rūpappaṭisaṃyutto vimokkho sāmiso vimokkho.

Katamo ca, bhikkhave, nirāmiso vimokkho? Arūpappaṭisaṃyutto vimokkho nirāmiso vimokkho.

in the fourth meditative absorption which is the purification of mindfulness by equanimity and is neither pleasant nor painful due to the subsiding of happiness and distress from previously letting go of pleasure and pain. This is called spiritual equanimity, monks.

"And what, monks, is the equanimity that is more spiritual than spiritual? For an awakened monk contemplating a mind free of desire, contemplating a mind free of hatred, and contemplating a mind free of delusion, equanimity arises. This is called an equanimity more spiritual than spiritual.

"And what, monks, is sensory freedom? Sensory freedom is freedom connected to dimensions of awareness tied to sensory things.

"And what, monks, is spiritual freedom? Spiritual freedom is freedom connected to dimensions of awareness that lack material form.

Katamo ca, bhikkhave, nirāmisā nirāmisataro vimokkho? Yo kho, bhikkhave, khīṇāsavassa bhikkhuno rāgā cittaṃ vimuttaṃ paccavekkhato, dosā cittaṃ vimuttaṃ paccavekkhato, mohā cittaṃ vimuttaṃ paccavekkhato uppajjati vimokkho, ayaṃ vuccati, bhikkhave, nirāmisā nirāmisataro vimokkhoti.

"And what, monks, is freedom that is more spiritual than spiritual? For an awakened monk contemplating a mind free of desire, contemplating a mind free of hatred, and contemplating a mind free of delusion, freedom arises. This is called a freedom more spiritual than spiritual."

FOUR IMMEASURABLES

We have begun to learn of the joy, freedom, and equanimity that arise when one relinquishes desire, hatred, and delusion. We turn now to certain highly valued experiences that emerge particularly when hatred and its many affiliates, such as resentment, anger, envy, and cruelty are given up. Hate, anger, and resentment erect barriers between us and others. When they are removed, one's perspective and scope of action become free of such barricades and become enlarged and expansive. What emerges from mindfulness techniques removing such constrictions are the four "immeasurables" or "sublime attitudes"—lovingkindness, compassion, sympathetic joy, and equanimity.

Lovingkindness—also translated as friendliness—is a natural state of good will one has toward others when one is free of anger, resentment, or hate toward them. The commentaries outline substantial spiritual exercises to remove these negative feelings so that "freedom of the loving mind" can arise.[1] *To be free of one's grudges, anger, resentment, thoughts of revenge, and the like is a kind of "liberation" in that one can move freely in the world mingling with all beings, open and present to who they are. One's mind is not tight, constricted, blinkered, or cut off. And others, sensing one's friendliness, respond in kind, making one still more free and expansive. Inasmuch as lovingkindness is a practice that is "immeasurable," one can forever grow in it, ever refining it in practice and ever finding more beings toward whom to feel it. It is a kind of universal altruism.*

Compassion is the wish that those suffering be rid of their suffering; it counters and removes cruelty and indifference. Sympathetic joy is finding happiness in others' success; it counters and removes discontent and envy. Finally, equanimity is balance and peace come what may; it quiets aversion and preference by attending to others with equality and impartiality. These, like lovingkindness, are practices that are immeasurable in scope and practice, and all liberate the mind.

In our selection, these four states are referred to as "sublime attitudes," or more literally, "divine abidings"(brahmavihāras), in that they are ways of living that are heavenly or divine. The passage tells the tale of a young Brahmin student, Subha, who is keen to know the way to heaven, the world of the god Brahma. (Brahma is a Hindu god, but he also is thought by Buddhists to dwell in a gentle, loving place in the heavens.) Subha asks the Buddha about this, and the Buddha replies that he knows all about the heavenly world of Brahma, and how to reach it. The way to do so is to "flood" or "pervade" one's mind—and, of course, heart—with each of the sublime attitudes and direct them to others first in one direction, then a second, and gradually working up to flooding beings in all directions with lovingkindness and the other immeasurables. This makes one's experience and activity open, spacious, and free. Heaven is not something one has to postpone to the afterlife; it can be achieved with a loving mind here and now.

Subha Sutta (excerpted from the Majjhima Nikāya ii.206-208)

Subho māṇavo todeyyaputto bhagavantaṃ etadavoca—sutaṃ metaṃ, bho gotama—samaṇo gotamo brahmānaṃ sahabyatāya maggaṃ jānātīti.

Taṃ kiṃ maññasi, māṇava, āsanne ito naḷakāragāmo, na yito dūre naḷakāragāmo ti?
Evaṃ, bho, āsanne ito naḷakāragāmo, na yito dūre naḷakāragāmo ti.

Taṃ, kiṃ maññasi māṇava, idhassa puriso naḷakāragāme jātavaddho tamenaṃ naḷakāragāmato tāvadeva avasaṭaṃ naḷakāragāmassa maggaṃ puccheyyuṃ; siyā nu kho, māṇava, tassa purisassa naḷakāragāme jātavad-

The Brahmin student Subha, son of Todeyya, asked the Buddha: "Master Gotama, I have heard it said that 'The renouncer Gotama knows the road to the company of the god Brahma.'"

"What do you think, young man, is the village of Nalakara located near, not far, from here?"

"Yes, sir, Nalakara village is near and not far from here."

"What do you think, young man, suppose a person born and raised in the village of Nalakara had just arrived from Nalakara village and was asked about the road to Nalakara. Do you think, young man, that a person born and raised in Nalakara village

dhassa naḷakāragāmassa maggaṃ puṭṭhassa dandhāyitattaṃ vā vitthāyitattaṃ vā ti?

No hidaṃ, bho gotama.

Taṃ kissa hetu?

Amu hi, bho gotama, puriso naḷakāragāme jātavaddho. Tassa sabbāneva naḷakāragāmassa maggāni suviditānīti.

Siyā nu kho, māṇava, tassa purisassa naḷakāragāme jātavaddhassa naḷakāragāmassa maggaṃ puṭṭhassa dandhāyitattaṃ vā vitthāyitattaṃ vāti, na tveva tathāgatassa brahmalokaṃ vā brahmalokagāminiṃ vā paṭipadaṃ puṭṭhassa dandhāyitattaṃ vā vitthāyitattaṃ vā. Brahmānañcāhaṃ, māṇava, pajānāmi brahmalokañca brahmalokagāminiñca paṭipadaṃ; yathāpaṭipanno ca brahmalokaṃ upapanno tañca pajānāmīti.

Sutaṃ metaṃ, bho gotama—samaṇo gotamo brahmānaṃ sahabyatāya maggaṃ

would have any hesitation or delay in replying about the road to Nalakara?"

"Of course not, Master Gotama."

"And why is that?"

"Because the person was born and raised in Nalakara village, sir, they are well acquainted with all roads to Nalakara."

"Still, young man, a person born and raised in Nalakara might hesitate or delay when asked about the road to Nalakara. But there is no hesitation or delay for the Buddha when asked about the heavenly world of Brahma or the path to the heavenly world of Brahma. Young man, I understand fully Brahma, the heavenly world of Brahma, and the pathway leading to the heavenly world of Brahma. And I understand the practice by which one attains the Brahma heaven."

"I have heard it said, Master Gotama, that 'The renouncer Gotama teaches the road to

desetīti. Sādhu me bhavaṃ gotamo brahmānaṃ sahabyatāya maggaṃ desetūti.

Tena hi, māṇava, suṇāhi, sādhukaṃ manasi karohi, bhāsissāmīti.

Evaṃ bho ti kho subho māṇavo todeyyaputto bhagavato paccassosi.

Bhagavā etadavoca—Katamo ca, māṇava, brahmānaṃ sahabyatāya maggo? Idha, māṇava, bhikkhu mettāsahagatena cetasā ekaṃ disaṃ pharitvā viharati, tathā dutiyaṃ, tathā tatiyaṃ, tathā catutthaṃ; iti uddhamadho tiriyaṃ sabbadhi sabbattatāya sabbāvantaṃ lokaṃ mettāsahagatena cetasā vipulena mahaggatena appamāṇena averena abyābajjhena pharitvā viharati.

Evaṃ bhāvitāya kho, māṇava, mettāya cetovimuttiyā yaṃ pamāṇakataṃ kammaṃ na

the company of Brahma.' It would be good if Gotama would teach me the road to the company of Brahma."

"Then listen attentively, young man, and I will speak."

"Yes, sir," replied the young Brahmin student Subha, son of Todeyya, to the Buddha.

The Buddha spoke: "What is the road to the company of Brahma? Now, young man, a monk lives having flooded a single direction with thoughts full of lovingkindness. Then a second direction, then a third, and then the fourth, and then above and below, and horizontally everywhere, he lives having flooded the entire world with thoughts full of lovingkindness, encompassing all beings, expansive, enlarged, immeasurable, without animosity, and free of ill will.

"When the freedom of the loving mind is practiced in this way, young man, no action

taṃ tatrāvasissati, na taṃ tatrāvatiṭṭhati. Seyyathāpi, māṇava, balavā saṅkhadhamo appakasireneva cātuddisā viññāpeyya evameva kho, bhāvitāya kho, māṇava, mettāya cetovimuttiyā yaṃ pamāṇakataṃ kammaṃ na taṃ tatrāvasissati, na taṃ tatrāvatiṭṭhati. Ayampi kho, māṇava, brahmānaṃ sahabyatāya maggo.

Puna caparaṃ, māṇava, bhikkhu karuṇāsahagatena cetasā . . . pe . . . muditāsahagatena cetasā . . . pe . . . upekkhāsahagatena cetasā ekaṃ disaṃ pharitvā viharati, tathā dutiyaṃ, tathā tatiyaṃ, tathā catutthaṃ; iti uddhamadho tiriyaṃ sabbadhi sabbattatāya sabbāvantaṃ lokaṃ karuṇāsahagatena cetasā . . . pe . . . muditāsahagatena cetasā . . . pe . . . upekkhāsahagatena cetasā vipulena mahaggatena appamāṇena averena abyābajjhena pharitvā viharati.

Evaṃ bhāvitāya kho, māṇava, upekkhāya cetovimuttiyā yaṃ pamāṇakataṃ kammaṃ

limited in scope remains there or persists there. Just as a powerful conch blower easily blasts news to the four directions, so too, young man, when freedom of the loving mind is practiced in this way, no action limited in scope remains or persists there. This is the road to the company of Brahma.

"So too, young man, a monk lives having flooded a single direction, then a second direction, then a third, and then the fourth, and then above and below, and horizontally everywhere with thoughts full of compassion . . . sympathetic joy . . . and equanimity. Having flooded the entire world with thoughts full of compassion . . . sympathetic joy . . . and equanimity, he lives encompassing all beings, expansive, enlarged, immeasurable, without animosity, and free of ill will.

"When the mind is freed by the practice of each of these up through equanimity in

na taṃ tatrāvasissati, na taṃ tatrāvatiṭṭhati. Seyyathāpi, māṇava, balavā saṅkhadhamo appakasireneva cātuddisā viññāpeyya; evameva kho, māṇava . . . pe . . . evaṃ bhāvitāya kho, māṇava, upekkhāya cetovimuttiyā yaṃ pamāṇakataṃ kammaṃ na taṃ tatrāvasissati, na taṃ tatrāvatiṭṭhati. Ayampi kho, māṇava, brahmānaṃ sahabyatāya maggo"ti.

Evaṃ vutte, subho māṇavo todeyyaputto bhagavantaṃ etadavoca—abhikkantaṃ, bho gotama, abhikkantaṃ, bho gotama! Seyyathāpi, bho gotama, nikkujjitaṃ vā ukkujjeyya, paṭicchannaṃ vā vivareyya, mūḷhassa vā maggaṃ ācikkheyya, andhakāre vā telapajjotaṃ dhāreyya—cakkhumanto rūpāni dakkhantīti—evamevaṃ bhotā gotamena anekapariyāyena dhammo pakāsito.

this way, young man, no action limited in scope remains there or persists there. Just as a powerful conch blower easily blasts news to the four directions, so too, young man, when the freedom of the mind that is equanimity is practised in this way, no action limited in scope remains there or persists there. This is the road to the company of Brahma."

When this was said, the Brahmin student Subha, son of Todeyya, replied to the Buddha: "Marvelous, Master Gotama, marvelous, Master Gotama! Master Gotama has illustrated the doctrine by various methods in exactly this way, having set upright what had been overturned, having revealed what had been hidden, having shown the way to one who was lost, or having held up an oil lamp in the darkness so that those with eyes may see that which can be seen."

AN UPWARD SPIRAL

This last brief chapter is a short teaching from another book of the Pali Canon, the Numerical Discourses (Aṅguttara Nikāya). I include it here because it suggests something quite subtle about how we work psychologically and how we begin to achieve freedom.

The teaching describes a spiral of conditions beginning with a person practicing virtuous conduct. Virtuous conduct means that one avoids killing, stealing, lying, sexual misconduct, and taking intoxicants. This teaching thus places mental development on a moral foundation. With the condition of not engaging in harmful thoughts and behavior, one will be free of the scratchy feeling of remorse that can include regret, guilt, shame, worry, and anxiety.

This begins an upward spiral. If one enjoys the absence of remorse, one need not then generate a further thought or intention to be delighted. In fact, generating an intention to be delighted (or joyful or calm or happy) tends not to be effective anyway: it is not as if we can bring delight into our lives by demanding that it appear or by forcing ourselves to feel it. Positive states arise as a result of conditions; we can't manufacture them by fiats of will, and the more we chase them the more elusive they become. Rather, they emerge, as this teaching suggests, when the mind is simply clear of fretting about oneself and worrying about whether one has been harming the world. Free of regrets, one is open to the moment one is in and can fully participate—and find delight—in it.

And so, the condition that starts the upward spiral is removal—by removing harmful actions and thoughts, one enjoys a free, clear, and easy mind that invites delight, and then joy, calm, happiness, and further states building on these. All of these are said to occur "in the nature of things" where phenomena flow naturally from one condition to another.

Delighted, joyful, calm, and pleasant experiences then give rise to the ability to concentrate and attend to experience. When one can attend to what is present without distortions, distractions, and agitations, one can begin to "know and see things as they truly are."

And when one knows and sees things as they truly are one grows disenchanted with them due to their impermanent and conditioned nature. Detaching from them makes it possible to know and see in a way that is free, with freedom being the ultimate aim of all practice.

Cetanā (Aṅguttara Nikāya v.2-4)

Sīlavato, bhikkhave, sīlasampannassa na cetanāya karaṇīyaṃ—avippaṭisāro me uppajjatūti. Dhammatā esā, bhikkhave, yaṃ sīlavato sīlasampannassa avippaṭisāro uppajjati.

Avippaṭisārissa, bhikkhave, na cetanāya karaṇīyaṃ—'pāmojjaṃ me uppajjatū'ti. Dhammatā esā, bhikkhave, yaṃ avippaṭisārissa pāmojjaṃ jāyati.

Pamuditassa, bhikkhave, na cetanāya karaṇīyaṃ—'pīti me uppajjatū'ti. Dhammatā esā, bhikkhave, yaṃ pamuditassa pīti uppajjati.

Pītimanassa, bhikkhave, na cetanāya karaṇīyaṃ—'kāyo me passambhatū'ti. Dhammatā esā, bhikkhave, yaṃ pītimanassa kāyo passambhati.

"Monks, one who is virtuous does not need the intention, *May I be without remorse*. For it is the nature of things, monks, that freedom from remorse arises for one who is virtuous, who has good conduct.

"Monks, one who is without remorse does not need the intention, *May delight arise in me*. For it is the nature of things, monks, that delight arises in one free of remorse.

"Monks, one who is delighted does not need the intention, *May joy arise in me*. For it is the nature of things, monks, that joy arises in the delighted.

"Monks, one who is joyful does not need the intention, *May my body calm down*. For it is the nature of things, monks, that one who is joyful has a calm body.

Passaddhakāyassa, bhikkhave, na cetanāya karaṇīyaṃ—'sukhaṃ vediyāmī'ti. Dhammatā esā, bhikkhave, yaṃ passaddhakāyo sukhaṃ vediyati.

Sukhino, bhikkhave, na cetanāya karaṇīyaṃ—'cittaṃ me samādhiyatū'ti. Dhammatā esā, bhikkhave, yaṃ sukhino cittaṃ samādhiyati.

Samāhitassa, bhikkhave, na cetanāya karaṇīyaṃ—'yathābhūtaṃ jānāmi passāmī'ti. Dhammatā esā, bhikkhave, yaṃ samāhito yathābhūtaṃ jānāti passati.

Yathābhūtaṃ, bhikkhave, jānato passato na cetanāya karaṇīyaṃ—'nibbindāmi virajjāmī'ti. Dhammatā esā, bhikkhave, yaṃ yathābhūtaṃ jānaṃ passaṃ nibbindati virajjati.

"Monks, one whose body is calm does not need the intention, *Let me feel happy.* For it is the nature of things, monks, that one with a calm body feels happy.

"Monks, one who feels happy does not need the intention, *Let my mind become concentrated.* For it is the nature of things, monks, that the mind of one who feels happy is concentrated.

"Monks, one who is concentrated does not need the intention, *Let me know and see things as they truly are*. For it is the nature of things, monks, that one who is concentrated knows and sees things as they truly are.

"Monks, one who knows and sees things as they truly are does not need the intention, *Let me become disenchanted and dispassionate*. For it is the nature of things, monks, that one knowing and seeing things as they truly are is disenchanted and dispassionate.

Nibbinnassa bhikkhave, virattassa na cetanāya karaṇīyaṃ—'vimuttiñāṇadassanaṃ sacchikaromī'ti. Dhammatā esā, bhikkhave, yaṃ nibbinno viratto vimuttiñāṇadassanaṃ sacchikaroti.

Iti kho, bhikkhave, nibbidāvirāgo vimuttiñāṇadassanattho vimuttiñāṇadassanānisaṃso; yathābhūtañāṇadassanaṃ nibbidāvirāgatthaṃ nibbidāvirāgānisaṃsaṃ; samādhi yathābhūtañāṇadassanattho yathābhūtañāṇadassanānisaṃso; sukhaṃ samādhatthaṃ samādhānisaṃsaṃ; passaddhi sukhatthā sukhānisaṃsā; pīti passaddhatthā passaddhānisaṃsā; pāmojjaṃ pītatthaṃ pītānisaṃsaṃ; avippaṭisāro pāmojjattho pāmojjānisaṃso; kusalāni sīlāni avippaṭisāratthāni avippaṭisārānisaṃsāni.

"Monks, one who is disenchanted and dispassionate does not need the intention, *Let me realize for myself a way of knowing and seeing that is free*. For it is the nature of things, monks, that one disenchanted and dispassionate realizes for oneself a way of knowing and seeing that is free.

"Monks, knowing and seeing in a way that is free is the aim and benefit of becoming disenchanted and dispassionate. Disenchantment and dispassion are the aim and benefit of knowing and seeing things as they really are. Knowing and seeing things as they really are is the aim and benefit of concentration. Concentration is the aim and benefit of feeling happy. Happiness is the aim and benefit of being calm. Being calm is the aim and benefit of joy. Joy is the aim and benefit of delight. Delight is the aim and

Iti kho, bhikkhave, dhammā dhamme abhisandenti, dhammā dhamme paripūrenti apārā pāraṃ gamanāyāti.

benefit of freedom from remorse. Freedom from remorse is the aim and benefit of virtue.

"It is just so, monks, that phenomena flow into phenomena and phenomena succeed phenomena for one going from one shore to the other."

NOTES ON THE TEXT AND TRANSLATION

To make this book as accessible and readable as possible, my translation aims for fidelity rather than literalness and follows English rather than Pali syntax. The Pali editions sometimes abbreviate lengthy repetitions, and I follow them, indicating abbreviations with ellipses. In several instances that I have noted, I added material that was abbreviated because the editions abbreviated material given at length in selections that were not excerpted here but are important for the meaning. Pali dialogues also tend to use more vocatives than we would in English, and I have omitted translating all of them.

The editions are those of the Chaṭṭha-Saṅgayana, Vipassana Research Institute (2018), available for free at https://tipitaka.org/. I made minimal changes in the editions presented here.

Additionally, for the text of "Two Kinds of Thoughts" (*Majjhima Nikāya* i.114–118; *suttanta* 19), I also consulted GRETIL (Göttingen Register for Electronic Texts in Indian Languages) for the digital version of the Pali Text Society, ed. V. Trenckner, London, 1988, input by the Dhammakaya Foundation, Thailand, 1989–1996. For "Teachings on Feelings," I consulted GRETIL's digital version of the *Saṃyutta Nikāya* (iv.204–237, *suttanta* 36), ed. Feer, London: Pali Text Society 1894, input by the Dhammakaya Foundation, Thailand, 2015. And for "An Upward Spiral," I consulted GRETIL's version of the *Aṅguttara Nikāya* (v.2–4), E. Hardy, London: Pali Text Society 1900, input by the Dhammakaya Foundation, Thailand, 1989–1996.

GLOSSARY

awakening, see *nirvana*

chains (saṃyojana): the bonds or fetters holding back spiritual progress. The five chains tethering us to the world of the senses are belief in autonomous individuality, doubt, clinging to mere rules and rituals, sensual desire, and ill will

clearly comprehending (sampajana, sampajañña): being fully attentive to the movements and activities of mind and body in ways that comprehend their myriad causes and effects

compassion (karunā): a practice of attention and freedom that counters cruelty and indifference; it is one of the four "immeasurables" or "divine abidings"; also translated as care, it is the longing that others' suffering cease

craving (taṇhā): the deep thirst or desire perpetuating suffering. It is one link in dependent arising and it is the Second Noble Truth, stated as the cause or origin of suffering

dependent arising (paṭiccasamuppāda): a twelve-fold analysis of moment-by-moment experience that shows the successive and sometimes mutual conditions of ignorance, habitual patterns, consciousness, name-and-form, the six senses, sensory contact, feeling, craving, attachment, becoming, aging-and-death, and birth

destructive predispositions (āsava): literally, the "oozings" or discharging of the four toxic dispositions—desire, craving for eternal existence, wrong views, and ignorance. One "free of the destructive predispositions" (*anāsava, khīṇāsava*) has attained nirvana

sublime attitudes, see *immeasurables*

distress (domanassa): a negative, dejected, and depressed mind. Distress is a feeling and a faculty for coming to things with a negative outlook. Its opposite is *somanassa* (see *happiness*)

dukkha: (1) painful valence or tone; (2) the suffering spoken of in the First Noble Truth, that includes the stress, misery, and sorrows of life, and the suffering underlying even pleasant experience insofar as it is transient and contingent on factors beyond our control

eightfold path (ariyo aṭṭhaṅgiko maggo): the Fourth Noble Truth and the way to end suffering via right view (understanding the Four Noble Truths), right intention (the intentions of letting things go, good will, and harmlessness), right speech (avoiding lying, slander, harsh speech, and idle chatter), right action (avoiding killing, stealing, and sexual misconduct), right livelihood (giving up wrong livelihoods that violate right action and speech), right effort (working to restrain and abandon unhealthy states and develop and maintain healthy ones), right mindfulness (the four applications of mindfulness), and right concentration (practicing advanced meditative absorptions)

equanimity (upekkhā): the mental balance and nonreactivity achieved through meditation wherein one does not swing back and forth between likes and dislikes. In some contexts, equanimity is a feeling; in other contexts, it can be seen as a faculty and a way of approaching the world. It is also an "immeasurable" or "sublime attitude," a practice of freedom in attending to others with balanced and impartial concern

feeling (vedanā): the category of affective valences or tones of experience, as well as certain experiences (thoughts, aptitudes, faculties) that have these valences

four noble truths (cattāri ariyasaccāni): (1) there is suffering (*dukkha*); (2) there is an origin of suffering, namely, craving; (3) suffering can cease, which is nirvana; and (4) the Eightfold Path is the way to end it

happiness (somanassa): literally, "good" or "happy" mind; mental pleasure; happiness;

gladness; it is also the faculty of having a positive outlook. Its opposite is *domanassa*, "negative" or "dejected" mind (see DISTRESS). Happiness is also a translation of SUKHA

habitual patterns (saṅkhāras): the prefiguring ways humans construct experience based on predispositions, past experience, and inclination. In Buddhist psychology, based on ignorance and biases, the habitual patterns condition how we perceive, feel, conceptualize, and construct each moment of awareness

immeasurables (appamāṇa): the four sublime attitudes or heavenly "abidings" that are the practices of lovingkindness, compassion, sympathetic joy, and equanimity. They are meditation practices that are measureless in that they can always be expanded further toward more and more beings, and with greater and greater refinement

joy (pīti): literally, a "lovely feeling"; elation. Joy is felt in the first two meditative absorptions, but drops out in the third. Joy can also be divided into sensory and spiritual forms

letting things go (nekkhamma): the renunciation or giving up of sensory attachments; it can replace its opposite, sense desires

lovingkindness (mettā): a practice of attention and freedom that counters anger and hate; it is one of the four "immeasurables" or "sublime attitudes"; also translated as "friendliness" and good will, it is the longing that others be happy

meditative absorptions (jhāna): four highly advanced states that involve deep and focused engagement with meditation objects

mindfulness (sati): close observation of what happens in us and to us, moment by moment, registering what occurs while not being drawn into it

name-and-form (nāmarūpa): categories of experience into mental and material processes: "name" refers to the processes of selecting out salient features in a field of perception and feeling and identifying them with labels, and "form" refers to the impingement or impact the material world makes in a field of perception

nirvana (nibbāṇa): the awakening or enlightenment experience of being free of desire, hatred, and delusion; the third of the Four Noble Truths, which is the ceasing of all suffering

pain, see *dukkha*

pleasure, see *sukha*

sensory (sāmisa): carnal, related to the body or the senses, referring to feelings; in contrast to "spiritual" (*nirāmisa*)

spiritual (nirāmisa): not sensory or carnal, not based on the body and its senses, referring to feelings; in contrast to "sensory" (*sāmisa*)

suffering, see *dukkha*

sukha: (1) pleasant valence or tone; (2) pleasure, happiness, ease, bliss, including higher states that have nothing to do with pleasant feeling

sympathetic joy (muditā): a practice of attention and freedom that counters discontent and envy; it is one of the four "immeasurables" or "sublime attitudes"; also translated as altruistic joy, its content is feeling happy at others' success

underlying tendencies (anusaya): deeply-rooted dispositions or proclivities, often unconscious, that drive our behavior; there are seven: desire, aversion, wrong views, conceit, doubt, craving for eternal existence, and ignorance

understanding (Pali, pajānato): a full and experiential grasp of the matter at hand that constitutes a type of wisdom going beyond mere intellectual or conceptual knowledge

NOTES

Introduction

1 See Lisa Feldman Barrett, *How Emotions are Made: The Secret Life of the Brain* (Boston: Mariner Books, 2018). She shows how the classical view that emotions are universal essences with single identifiable biological fingerprints is not supported by the neuroscientific evidence, though it might be intuitive to see them as such, and this view has enjoyed a long history in Western thought (in the work of Darwin, Ekman, and others).

2 Linguist Anna Wierzbicka argues that "English terms of emotion constitute a folk taxonomy, not an objective, culture-free analytical framework, so obviously we cannot assume that English words such as disgust, fear, or shame are clues to universal human concepts, or to basic

psychological realities." She argues that "while English is a language of global significance, it is not a neutral instrument or one that, unlike other languages, carves nature at its joints; and that if this is not recognized, English can at times become a conceptual prison" (*Imprisoned in English: The Hazards of English as a Default Language.* New York: Oxford University Press, 2014: 71, 4).

3 This is stated in the Pali commentaries, specifically at *Aṅguttara Nikāya Aṭṭhakathā* ii.282. Barrett also argues that noticing and categorizing is crucial to the category of emotion: "Your muscle movements and bodily changes become functional instances of emotion *only when you categorize them that way*, giving them new functions as experiences and perceptions. Without emotion concepts these new functions don't exist. They are only moving faces, beating hearts, circulating hormones, and so on" (*How Emotions are Made*, 133, italics in original).

4 *Majjhima Nikāya* i.55. Translations of the "Applications of Mindfulness Teaching" (*Sati-*

paṭṭhāna Sutta) can be found in Bhikkhu Bodhi's *In the Buddha's Words* (Somerville, MA: Wisdom Publications, 2015):281–290, in Sarah Shaw's *Buddhist Meditation* (London: Routledge, 2006), 76–85; and in Nyanasatta Thera work at https://www.accesstoinsight.org/lib/authors/nyanasatta/wheel019.html. Scholars translate this term variously, such as the "foundations" and "establishments" of mindfulness.

5 *Aṅguttara Nikāya* iv.414.

Two Kinds of Thoughts

1 On the freedom found in giving up attachment to a notion of self or enduring personal identity, see *How to Lose Yourself: An Ancient Guide to Letting Go*, translations by Jay Garfield, Maria Heim, and Robert Sharf, Princeton: Princeton University Press, 2025.

2 As for example, Judson Brewer, *The Craving Mind: From Cigarettes to Smartphones to Love—Why We Get Hooked and How We Can Break Bad Habits*, New Haven: Yale University Press, 2017.

3 The teaching continues for another page or so after this, describing how with this composed mind, Siddhattha was able to achieve the advanced meditative absorptions and finally, nirvana.

Teachings on Feelings

1 Literally, "internal" and "external"; the commentary says that internal feeling refers to one's own feelings, and external feelings are those of others (*Saṃyutta Aṭṭhakāthā* iii.74).

2 See, for example, J. David Cresswell, "Accepting Discomfort Could Help You Thrive," *Scientific American*, February 2024: 72–73.

3 *Majjhima Nikāya* i.293: "Friend, one perceives what one feels; and one cognizes what one perceives. Therefore, these phenomena are mixed, not separate. It is not possible to disentangle fully these phenomena to make their distinctions entirely understood."

4 *Saṃyutta Nikāya* iv.127.

5 Positive psychologist Mihaly Csikszentmihalyi refers to "flow experiences" as deep immersions in an experience in which time, self, and ordinary perception fall away.

6 The text reads simply "in breath and out breath," which I have interpreted as labored breathing in and out. Modern scholars are divided on whether the texts mean that inhalation and exhalation cease entirely (and exactly what that would entail) in the fourth meditative absorption. Thanks to Sarah Shaw for her help with this.

7 These four classes refer to the traditional orders of Indian society.

8 This passage quotes the second half of "Being Alone" above, which the edited text and I have abbreviated.

9 A Chinese parallel version of this *sutta* goes further than the 108 we find in the Pali to say that there are "innumerable *vedanās*" (Bhikkhu Anālayo, *Deepening Insight: Teachings on*

Vedanā in the Early Buddhist Discourses. Onalaska, WA: Pariyatti, 2021). This approach to the infinity of potential feelings and emotions resonates with the spirit of the Pali text.

10 The question of how such elevated experiences beyond feeling may still be seen as *sukha* is taken up by Grzegorz Polok, "The Pleasure of Not Experiencing Anything: Some Reflections on Consciousness in the Context of the Early Buddhist Nikāyas," *Religions* 2023, *14*(11), 1–25. The author connects these experiences to "flow experiences" (see n.5).

11 My translation condenses some of the repetition here.

12 Brahmins are the priestly class of Hinduism. "Ascetics" refers to yogis, monastics, or religious seekers from many early sects and groups.

13 My translation fills in an abbreviation in the text referring to the four senses not named: hearing, smelling, tasting, and touching. In Buddhism, there is a sixth sense, the "mind sense" that takes input from the other five.

14 These become eighteen because each of the three modes of approach are multiplied by the six senses.

15 These become thirty-six because each is multiplied by the six senses.

16 There is considerable abbreviation of the repetition in the Pali passage that I have omitted in the translation.

Four Immeasurables

1 "Freedom of the loving mind" is my slightly free translation of *mettāya cetovimuttiyā*, the "liberation of the heart/mind by lovingkindness." As in many ancient traditions, heart and mind are often translated with the same word (here *ceto*). The key idea is that freedom comes from practicing love. The most substantial commentarial treatment of these spiritual exercises is the 5th century text *Visuddhimagga* by Buddhaghosa (see Bhikkhu Ñāñamoli, trans. *The Path of Purification*, Onalaska, WA: Pariyatti, 1991, chapter 9). For an analysis of these exercises which discusses their practices connecting

love, attention, and freedom, see Maria Heim, "Buddhaghosa on the Phenomenology of Love and Compassion," in J. Ganeri, *The Oxford Handbook of Indian Philosophy*, Oxford University Press, 2017, pp. 171–189.

FURTHER READING

The Pali Canon

An accessible and helpful collection of teachings can be found in Bhikkhu Bodhi, trans. *In the Buddha's Words: An Anthology of Discourses from the Pāli Canon*. Somerville, MA: Wisdom Publications, 2015.

Full translations of the collections from which the selections in this book are drawn can be found in Bhikkhu Bodhi, trans. *The Connected Discourses of the Buddha: A Translation of the Saṃyutta Nikāya*. Boston: Wisdom Publications, 2000; Bhikkhu Bodhi, trans. *The Numerical Discourses of the Buddha: A Translation of the Aṅguttara Nikāya*. Somerville, MA: Wisdom Publications, 2012; and Bhikkhu Ñāṇamoli and Bhikkhu Bodhi, trans. *The Middle Length Discourses of the Buddha: A Translation of the*

Majjhima Nikāya. Somerville, MA: Wisdom Publications, 2001.

An excellent translation and discussion of many of the *vedanā* teachings from both the Pali and Chinese recensions can be found in Bhikkhu Anālayo, *Deepening Insight: Teachings on Vedanā in the Early Buddhist Discourses*. Onalaska, WA: Pariyatti, 2021.

Useful translations of many Pali texts can be found on the website: www.accesstoinsight.org.

For a superb summary of the Noble Eightfold Path based on the Pali Canon, see Bhikkhu Bodhi, *The Noble Eightfold Path*. Onalaska, WA: BPS Pariyatti, 1994.

Buddhist Meditation

A thoroughly discussed and accessible collection of Pali texts on meditation practices can be found in Sarah Shaw's *Buddhist Meditation: An Anthology of Texts from the Pāli Canon*. London: Routledge, 2006.

Nyanaponika Thera's *The Heart of Buddhist Meditation*. London: Rider & Co., 1962, provides a translation and interpretation of the four applications of mindfulness.

An excellent guide to the kinds of meditation discussed in this book is Shaila Catherine's *The Jhānas: A Practical Guide to Deep Meditative States*. New York: Wisdom Publications, 2024.

Emotion and Feeling

On contemporary scientific approaches to emotion and feeling, see: Lisa Feldman Barrett's *How Emotions are Made: The Secret Life of the Brain*. Boston: Mariner Books, 2018, which offers some of the latest neuroscientific understanding of emotions.

Psychiatrist and neuroscientist Judson Brewer puts his research on addiction and anxiety in conversation with Buddhist mindfulness practice in *The Craving Mind*, New Haven: Yale University Press, 2017, and *Unwinding Anxiety*, Avery, 2021.

ACKNOWLEDGMENTS

Many thanks to Rob Tempio for including this book in the Ancient Wisdom for Modern Readers series, and to Chloe Coy and Eva Jaunzems for their hard work on it. I am grateful for the many helpful suggestions of both anonymous reviewers, whose care and attention made this a much better book. Thank you to Amherst College for the Spring sabbatical in 2024 that gave me air to breathe and time to work.

I feel tremendous gratitude to Jay Garfield for his careful and critical reading of the manuscript and his many suggestions to make it better, to say nothing of his generous collegiality as my colleague in the Happy

Valley for well over two decades. Sarah Shaw has taught me a lot about translating in general and Buddhist meditation in particular. I appreciate Bernat Font Clos and conversations we've had that have forced me to think with more depth about *vedanā*.

Finally, I always recall with warmth Charlie Hallisey as my first and main teacher of Pali. It is to him that this book is dedicated.